To Lucy
Good luck with your eCommerce Mash

eCommerce MasterPlan
YOUR 5 STEPS TO SUCCESSFUL ONLINE SELLING

Chloë **Thomas**

KERNU

Praise for
eCommerce MasterPlan

Chloë has done the impossible – condensed a massively complex and detailed subject into a crisp clear set of "To Do" lists with masses of live examples. I tried very hard but could not find anything she had left out.

Anyone running an eCommerce business will relate to so much of this book and get the inspiration to get on and improve their business almost immediately.

In 12 years of running an eCommerce business, I have found that just as you crack one new method of digital marketing, two more grow in its place. This book seems to get a grip of all the methods and allows you to conquer them in a manageable way.

If you are just starting on the eCommerce route, congratulations, you have found the Bible – I suggest you read Step 2 (How to build the right website) very thoroughly, right now!

Mark Ashley Miller, Founder, The Present Finder

This is the Bible to Website Management and Marketing 101. A good bookshelf addition for all dot.com dinosaurs, successful online managers, web entrepreneurs or total novices that need a no-nonsense straight to the point read of where to start and how.

I myself have been in this industry now for twelve years and it's always good to go back to the basics and refresh your own learnings - that's why I love this book.

Chloë Thomas shows you step-by-step how to build and manage your online business. She strips back to the core of what you are trying to achieve and demonstrates that it takes work, but it's much easier than you thought. Easy and enjoyable to read, with a clear a plan of action and totally applicable to today.

Maxine Duncan, Online Commercial Manager La Senza UK

eCommerce can be a minefield of abbreviations, technical terms and (like IT) a complex journey that would scare most people off creating and marketing a website.

The *eCommerce MasterPlan* by Chloë, an experienced eCommerce professional, breaks down many of the uncertainties of the ecommerce world. Understanding your business model as identified in the first Step is key and following the simple worksheets will really set you up for success and help you plan properly.

Throughout the *eCommerce MasterPlan* relevance is put on the importance of content being King. Plus, one small step that is planned is better than jumping in feet first with multiple ideas that don't get the attention needed. Chloë has also laid bare the fundamentals of running a web site, going out to tender with documents to make life easier and the key components of driving traffic to a website.

This book has something for everyone, whether a novice entering the world of eCommerce or someone like myself who has worked in eCommerce for many years. There is a takeaway for everyone.

This eCommerce master class not only covers the core elements you would expect but goes one step further; highlighting how to work out ROI, and giving simple examples that actually make sense. Plus, it's packed with ideas that you will be able to apply to your everyday planning, implementation and review of digital marketing.

A great read and followed up by a training course that will keep your mind bubbling for hours to come.

Lee Carpenter-Johnson, E-commerce director, Galactic Online

Acknowledgements

Whilst the actual writing of this book has only taken two and a half months, it has taken many years to build up the knowledge I needed to write it. So I would like to thank everyone I have worked with, clients and colleagues, as all of them have in some way or another helped me along the path that has led to this book.

Worthy of a name check are Cathy Burman, Jim McDowell, Eleanor Power, and John Beale. Thank you all for your guidance and the education you have given me; it has been invaluable.

My team at indiumonline are quite frankly awesome, so thank you Anton, Rachel, Will, and Fenella for holding the fort and looking after all our great clients while I have been writing.

Thank you to Sarah Williams at The Book Consultancy for making the whole writing and publishing process so easy. And to Paul Avins and the F10 team for all their help and advice this year.

Finally, I would like to say a massive thank you to Mum, Dad, Rob, Will and all my family and friends.

Thank you.

Chloë Thomas

Saturday 14th July, 2012

Contents

Introduction	**1**
Why an eCommerce MasterPlan?	
How to Use this Book	**5**
Section 1: The 5 Steps	**7**

Step 1: What Sort of eCommerce Business Are You? — 9
Which of the seven eCommerce Business Structures does your business fit into? What sort of product range do you have, and what is your USP? Once you have the answer to these questions you can start building your eCommerce MasterPlan.

Step 2: The First Core Foundation: — 23
How to build the right website
The website is the most important part of any eCommerce business. What sort of website do you need? How do you build it quickly and effectively? How to find the right PiggyBack website. Plus, avoid conversion blockers.

Step 3: The Second Core Foundation: — 37
Cost, profit and growth
To build the basis for future profit and growth, you need to get a handle on the key numbers in an eCommerce business. That is the Margin, the ROI, and the Scale. Then you know what you need to achieve.

Step 4: The Third Core Foundation: — 51
Products and promotions
Once you know the numbers, you can start organising what your products are going to be, and promotions sit very closely with your product decisions. How many products do you need? What promotions are you going to run? What mix do you need?

Step 5: I Have Built It: Why haven't they come?   61
(aka Marketing!)
The first 4 Steps culminate in the creation of your marketing plan. It's the marketing plan that will bring you your customers, and make them spend. Here we go through how to take the outcomes of the other 4 Steps and build them into a marketing plan.

Section 2: Key Online Marketing Methods

Content Marketing   81
For some of the eCommerce business structures, content is at the heart of their online marketing. For others it is a very useful tool. The key is in getting organised.

Email Marketing   91
The key tool every eCommerce business needs to master. It will keep your customers buying from you, it will drive your sales, and it will build your relationship with those customers.

Social Media Marketing   109
Increasingly important for every business because it impacts in so many ways. Social Media can build brand awareness, activate offline marketing, distribute your content, power your search traffic, and much more.

Brand Awareness Marketing   125
If brand or customer base are your USPs you need to work on building brand awareness. There are thousands of ways to do this – how do you work out how it should be done for your business?

Offline Marketing   133
To build an eCommerce business you can't just look online for your marketing – offline is still very powerful.

Search Marketing   145
If you can get search marketing working for you, then you build a solid foundation of sales – that just keeps coming in. But it's getting ever more complex. How can you build your search marketing so it keeps working for you, no matter what Google does?

PPC (Pay Per Click) Marketing   159
The quickest way to get sales online. Not as easy as it looks, though – success is in the optimisation, and how you build it to start with.

Remarketing   173
The newest kid on the block – it can improve the performance of all your marketing.

Partnership Marketing   **183**
A clever, low-cost way to build your business, so long as you can find the right people to partner with.

What next?   **191**

Introduction

Why an *eCommerce MasterPlan*?

eCommerce is a huge, growing industry. In the UK last year it grew by 16%, whilst Europe remains the biggest eCommerce marketplace. North America is catching up, and the eCommerce market in the Middle East grew by 45% last year.

Despite its size and maturity (in some markets) there is no roadmap for success. There is no easy-to-follow guide that will help eCommerce businesses succeed. It's that gap that I hope *eCommerce MasterPlan* will help to fill.

What is *eCommerce MasterPlan* based on?

Since 2001, I have been working in direct marketing, and since 2004 I have been directly involved with the structures and marketing of eCommerce businesses. At the last count I have been directly involved with the marketing of over 50 eCommerce businesses, some as a member of staff and some as a consultant. I have project managed more than 15 eCommerce website builds or rebuilds, and advised on many more. I have helped eCommerce businesses launch, go international, and helped high street retailers launch online. Unfortunately I have also seen them close or go under.

I have sold everything from high street fashion, to books, to holidays. In all that time, I have barely seen two businesses approach eCommerce in the same way, and I have frequently come across businesses avoiding a marketing method that holds the key to their success, or holding on to one that is doing them no favours at all.

What I have learnt along the way is that there are some clear structures that, when followed, invariably lead to success, and some great big potholes that, if you know about in advance, are really easy to avoid.

eCommerce MasterPlan is based on all I have learnt from being immersed in eCommerce for the last eight years. I believe it provides the blueprint, the roadmap, the Master Plan for the success of every eCommerce business. If you follow the 5 Steps outlined in this book you will build an eCommerce business that will succeed. And you will get there faster.

The 5 Steps are based on the thousands of conversations I have had with eCommerce business owners about the problems and successes they are having with their business. These are conversations with people who either:

- have a successful business but want to take it to the next level of success
- have a great idea for an eCommerce business but can't work out where or how to start
- have a business that should be doing well, but just doesn't seem to be taking off in the way they think it should.

If you are reading this book, you are almost certainly in one of those positions yourself – and this book will help you get started and take your business to the next level.

What is the *eCommerce MasterPlan* in under 300 Words?

Simply, the *eCommerce MasterPlan* is a five-step plan that will show you your recipe for success.

Step 1

One of the fundamental problems I see again and again with eCommerce businesses is that they don't know what they are trying to be.

There are just seven eCommerce Business Structures: by the end of Step 1 you will know which you are. You will also identify your USP and your Product Range Scope – once you know these three things, building your Master Plan is simple.

Step 2

At the heart of every eCommerce business is a great website. Here I'll explain how to get the right website for your business. This is an area that can make or break your business. So follow Step 2 to make sure you are one of the lucky ones.

Step 3

Every eCommerce business should be built to drive a profit, and you can build that in from Day One if you get the numbers right. Step 3: Cost, Profit and Growth will show you how.

Step 4

An eCommerce business needs something to sell, and you need to keep optimising those products. In Step 4, I'm going to show you how to keep your products performing.

Together, Steps 2, 3, and 4 are the Core Foundations of a successful eCommerce business. Get them right and the rest will be easy.

Step 5

Step 1 identified what sort of eCommerce business you are; that will help identify what marketing is going to work for you. Steps 2–4 built the foundation of the business ready for sales – and marketing is going to bring those to you. Step 5 will show you how to build your marketing plan, and what should be in it.

How to Use this Book

At the heart of the *eCommerce MasterPlan* is an understanding of what sort of eCommerce business you are running; so reading the first section and getting to grips with Step 1 is really rather critical.

After that, if you're an established eCommerce business, then you can get away with skipping to Step 5 to understand what the essential marketing methods for your type of eCommerce Business are. Then you can read up on the relevant marketing methods for you in the later sections. But, at some point, please do read Steps 2, 3, and 4 as you will learn vitally useful information to help you grow your business.

If you are new to eCommerce, then I highly recommend you work through all the Steps in order before diving into the individual marketing sections.

Once you have worked through the key areas for you, then the whole book is structured so you can easily dip in to the right part for you when you need it.

Ecommerce and online marketing are constantly changing, so the book is designed to help you take the right approach no matter what changes. Of course, though, you need to keep up to date with what's happening and how to use each of the tools: that's where eCommerceMasterPlan.com comes in, and throughout the book you'll find the following symbols when there's useful content available for you online:

WORKBOOK
I have created a series of workbooks to help you make the most of each section – so make sure you download them to work through alongside the sections. If you want to get the workbook for the whole book right now, then just go to eCommerceMasterPlan.com/Free.

DOWNLOAD...
I have also put a lot of useful templates on the website ready for you to download and use. Please do make the most of them when you see this logo!

WEBSITE
When there's some great extra content that will help you on the website we've used this logo.

Enjoy!

Section 1:
The 5 Steps

Step 1: What Sort of eCommerce Business Are You?

Before you start to build your eCommerce MasterPlan, you need to understand what sort of business you are building. By the end of this step you will know the answer to the three questions that sit at the heart of any eCommerce business:

- **What is your eCommerce Business Structure?**
- **What is the scope of your Product Range?**
- **What is your USP (unique selling proposition)?**

The answers to these three questions will impact on everything you do with your business, from systems, to products, to customer service, and marketing.

WORKBOOK
You can download the workbook for this section at
ecommerceMasterPlan.com/Free

Introducing the Seven eCommerce Business Structures

Not all eCommerce businesses are the same, and not all successful eCommerce businesses are the same. However, all the successful ones do fit into similar moulds. By consciously building your business based on one of these structures, you will build a better business faster.

We have identified that successful eCommerce businesses follow one of seven business structures:

1. **Online Only**
   the only way to see the products is online

2. **Mail Order**
   a transactional website plus a printed catalogue, and possibly one or two physical stores

3. **Big Bricks and Clicks**
   lots of physical stores and an eCommerce website

4. **Boutique Bricks and Clicks**
   just one or two physical locations plus the eCommerce website

5. **Mainstream PiggyBack**
   using the likes of Amazon or eBay to market the products, with no website of their own

6. **Niche PiggyBack**
   where sellers of similar products come together to market more easily, usually retaining their own blog or eCommerce site elsewhere too. The craft world (Etsy, Folksy), Hotels (hotels.com, laterooms.com), jewellery (Boticca), and Books (abebooks.co.uk) are good examples.

7. **Full Multichannel**
   Using multiple shops, catalogues, and eCommerce – by far the most complex and most difficult to achieve and run (e.g. Bravissimo, Crew Clothing, Next).

If your eCommerce business is to be successful it needs to fit into one of these seven structures. Over the years it may progress between them – so you may start on a Niche PiggyBack structure, move to an Online Only, and finally a Boutique Bricks and Clicks. For companies in non-PiggyBack structures, you may end up on eBay, Amazon or similar as an additional route to market – we will look at that as part of Partnering when we come to discussing your marketing mix.

Our Seven Core eCommerce Business Structures

Before we dive in you'll notice there's no mention of call centres so far, or of taking orders by phone. For customer service reasons, ANY eCommerce business should be ready and willing to take a call from a customer and an order over the phone if necessary. So it's not (and shouldn't be) a separate factor in defining which business structure you have.

To help you understand the separate eCommerce Business Structures, we've explained each below with an example plus the key challenges for businesses that have that structure.

Online Only

A business where the only route to purchase is online is the most straightforward of our structures. There are no catalogue mailings to new or existing customers, and no physical store for people to buy in either. But the business does take orders over the phone.

Examples: asos.com, lookfantastic.com, Made.com

Biggest challenge for the Online Only eCommerce Business:
- Customer recruitment

Mail Order

This is a business where a key part of the sales is driven by catalogue mailings.

Here, we're defining a catalogue as a paper mailing, sent to a defined list (of customers or prospective customers), that includes all the product details and product prices so customers can place their order straight away, without going elsewhere for more information.

Examples: Boden, House of Bath, Lands End

Biggest challenges for the Mail Order eCommerce Business:
- Understanding the joint role of catalogues and online marketing to bring customers to the business
- Getting customers to order via the website (usually much more cost-effective for the business)

Bricks and Clicks

Bricks and clicks is any business that has physical stores as well as its eCommerce website, but has no mailing catalogue. These could be high street stores, retail park stores, or stores in obscure locations. But they must be physical locations in which consumers can buy the products.

There is a lot of diversity among this group so we've split them into two sections. When a business goes from having one or two shops to having more than that, the systems and structures for the business fundamentally change. To take account of this, we have divided these eCommerce Bricks and Clicks businesses into those with three or more stores, and those with only one or two.

– Big Bricks and Clicks

Big Bricks and Clicks are companies with chains of stores (3+ stores) – either regionally or nationally.

For these businesses, the shop has almost always come before the website, so there will have been some real business structure plan in creating processes for the fulfilment of online orders and for the creation of the product information around which to build the website (in a shop you rarely need a picture of the item, or a written description of it).

Example: Argos, Boots, Topshop

Biggest challenge for the Big Bricks and Clicks eCommerce Business:
- Fully integrating the stores and website – people and systems

– Boutique Bricks and Clicks

Companies with one or two physical locations, usually regionally deployed.

Sometimes these businesses start with a shop and then decide to sell online as well, but for many of them it has actually happened the other way round!

The successful ones are usually businesses focused on a clear niche, be it a clothing boutique with a certain style, or a haberdashery store. So usually they sell something that is hard to find.

Example: Boswells, Burford Needlecraft, Brownsfashion.com

Biggest challenge for the Boutique Bricks and Clicks eCommerce Business:
- Keeping the shop and the online business working well – it's a tough juggling act, especially at the beginning

PiggyBack

As with the Bricks and Clicks eCommerce businesses, we've divided this sector in two.

PiggyBacking is the use of someone else's infrastructure to get your products to market. That infrastructure usually includes:

- website and payment system
- marketing
- brand awareness
- customer database

So all the piggybacking business has to do is find the products, process, and send the orders.

The benefits to the eCommerce business can be huge:
- Speed – you can get your products in front of prospective buyers within minutes, and be generating sales within hours
- Investment – you don't need to build a website or a payment system – so the set-up costs are negligible
- Legal – all the legal faff of selling online is dealt with by the company whose site you are piggy backing (e.g. PCI DSS, Cookie Laws, 3D Secure, etc.)

Possibly the biggest benefit is that you can use this system to build and test your business. You can work out what sells, what things need to be priced at, and you can build up a customer database ready for when you go out on your own.

Mainstream PiggyBack

This is using sites like Amazon and eBay, where you are tapping into their huge infrastructure and customer base.

You can sell pretty much anything through these organisations, and you don't need your own website at all.

Biggest challenge for the Mainstream PiggyBack eCommerce Business:
- Deciding when/if you should create your own website

– Niche PiggyBacking

In several sectors, there are niche sites where you can PiggyBack. For example:

- Hotels and travel – laterooms.com, hotels.com, etc.
- Craft and vintage – Etsy, Folksy, Boticca
- Books – AbeBooks

Rather than getting you in front of the world, these niche businesses get you in front of segments of consumers who want your products.

Usually, in these niche PiggyBacking arrangements, the consumer's visibility of you as the seller is far greater – so it's more obvious that they are buying from you, not from the site you are piggy backing.

In most cases, you'll also want your own website, because the products you are selling gain in value depending on the amount of information you are able to provide to the consumer. So, if you are an Etsy seller, you want to have your own blog with more information about what you do and examples of previous work and new projects. If you are a hotel, you want your own site to answer the questions you can't fit into the Laterooms formats.

And many niche piggy backers will also be selling via eBay and Amazon.

Biggest challenge for the Niche PiggyBack eCommerce Business:
- Building a good reputation on the Niche PiggyBack site
- Choosing the right site to PiggyBack on

Full Multichannel

Multichannel is the merger of Mail Order and Bricks and Clicks: a business that has a catalogue, and a website and stores. This is by far the most difficult to succeed at because each of the three channels has different demands:

- In a catalogue the prices are printed, so you are stuck with them for some time – one month, three months, a year. In retail, you can change prices overnight – launch a sale, a new promotion, etc. Online you can launch a promotion in seconds.
- In a catalogue you state several hundred products that are available to buy over a period of time. If the stock doesn't come in, you have issues. In retail and online you just remove the product.
- You have got stock in lots of places – how do you integrate that?
- There are very few systems that do all three well – you are likely to end up compromising
- Customer service can be a real issue, and customer expectations keep getting higher

Many retail businesses have failed because they decided to be multichannel but got it wrong. Few businesses have succeeded in becoming true multichannel.

Example: Bravissimo, Next, Screwfix

Biggest challenge for the Multichannel eCommerce Business:
- Keeping the needs of customers across the channels satisfied – building a seamless experience.

What Is the Scope of Your Product Range?

Before we dive into identifying your USP (unique selling proposition), we need to explore the scope of your product range. This isn't the number of products you sell, rather how varied they are.

As well as fitting into one of the seven eCommerce Business Structures, the strongest eCommerce performers usually have a product range that is at either end of the product range scale:

PRODUCT RANGE SCALE

◄──── Niche ──────────────────── Department Store ────►

At the Niche End of the Scale

Niche sellers focus on a single product category – tea towels, sailing holidays, ladies' shoes – and they create and edit the perfect range of that product in such a way that, if you want that product, you know they are the only person to go to, e.g. classicsailing.com, thevacuumbagshop.co.uk, batterystation.co.uk, todryfor.com.

But don't assume that being niche means you can't be big.

One of the fastest-growing eCommerce businesses at the moment is World Stores with a turnover of over £35m, and they have built their business on niches. They identify ranges of keywords that have a high search volume, with a low amount of competition from other providers and where they know they can offer a better product range and customer service than the other providers do. For each niche, they build a new website (on a central platform). Currently they have websites for products as diverse as garden sheds and chimineas, to rowing machines and cots - over 70 websites in all.

Compatible eCommerce Business Structures:
All of them!

At the Department Store End of the Scale

Department Store sellers stock EVERYTHING. Like a traditional high street department store their website is packed with all kinds of different products, but even more products than the traditional department stores could ever possibly stock. So John Lewis is less of an online department store than Tesco, Amazon or Next. The aim of firms at this end of the scale is to become their customers' go-to destination every time those customers think of buying online.

Compatible eCommerce Business Structures:
Online Only, Mail Order, Big Bricks and Clicks, Full Multichannel

In the Middle of the Product Range Scale

The businesses in the middle, therefore, are not the obvious place for the consumer to go to for what they want. They are not the default "I bet Amazon have it" choice, nor are they likely to come up when someone searches for their product. So they must work much harder to differentiate themselves and ensure they build and retain a good customer base and/or a strong brand.

However many products you choose to stock, you should edit those products for your customers – have a basic, better, and best of each thing – and nothing more. Consumers really appreciate being helped to find the right option. Plus it will help you keep inventory down.

So at either end of the scale your strategic plan is fairly straightforward: every decision you make is tailored towards seeing how well it fits with your overall proposition. However, it's VERY hard to start off as a Department Store. These eCommerce businesses have grown so widely in order to maximise their customer base and brand power – so it's almost impossible to enter the market here.

You should now be able to see which of the seven eCommerce Business Structures your business should fit into. That's great, because now you know the foundations you are building your business on and that makes all the strategy decisions to come much easier.

You Know What You Are: What next?

Unfortunately, just knowing what you are isn't enough: you now need to differentiate your business from your competition.

Differentiate – Find Your USP

There are millions of eCommerce websites that your prospective customers can buy from. There are probably hundreds of thousands of eCommerce websites on which they can buy similar products to yours. So you need to create a reason for them to buy from you – and to keep buying from you; something that differentiates you from all the other websites out there (and from the shops and catalogues they could buy from too).

By differentiating yourself you create a Unique Selling Proposition (USP) for your business, the unique reason customers will keep buying from you rather than anyone else. For your USP to be effective, you need to be really good at whatever you choose to differentiate in, be better than the competition: you need to be 'best in class'.

In the 1960s, Michael Porter defined three generic strategies for business:

- Cost (how well in control of your costs you are, which relates directly to how much you charge)
- Niche (a customer group you will focus on)
- Differentiation (products, service, brand, customer intimacy).

It is still true today that every business needs to decide on which of these three it will primarily focus on, but in the 21st Century no company can afford to ignore their cost base or not understand their core customer base. So a USP needs to be more than just one of these three generic strategies.

Saying that, the three generic strategies above are a good place to start, and it's crucial to understand if either of the first two is important to your business.

Take a look at your sector. There are sectors filled with 'commodity' products - here you have to be price competitive (think TVs and Laptops). Now that we can easily sell globally, even the most specialist market is big enough to have multiple eCommerce sites serving it.

So:

- are you all about getting the costs under control so you can beat everyone on price (see Tesco)?
- are you going to focus on a single customer segment? Or consumer need?
- are you neither of these?

Whichever you have answered yes to, you still need a further point of differentiation for your USP and make sure it's compatible to your sector.

What Are the Successful eCommerce USPs?

There are broadly seven USPs that work well. The first three are the most powerful (the hardest for your competition to copy):

- Customer Service – this aligns closely with Delivery and Returns, but is much more than getting the parcel out correctly. It's about all the ways you communicate with a customer. You need to be responding within hours (not days) to queries on Facebook, Twitter, email, etc. And you need to make it really easy for customers to do business with you. Going the extra mile is also critical: when one of International Dance Supplies' Greek customer's parcels didn't arrive in time for their dance school show, one of the International Dance Supplies team hopped on a plane with replacements! Are you willing to do that?
- Knowledge & Information – this is the value-add over the product. Can the customer be 100% sure the item on your site is the one they want? Have you included the length of the skirt? The batteries that the MP3 player takes? And it's more than that – do you show customers how to use your products? Videos, articles, guides: they are all key. Your site needs to be the centre for information on your products.
- Customer Base – this is one differentiator that is VERY hard and VERY expensive for your competition to steal. It's also expensive to build; you need a huge list of customers that will consistently buy from you – think Amazon or John Lewis.
- Brand – can be closely linked to building a big customer base. Be front of mind, be the only choice for what you are offering. Own your industry. Online Auction = eBay, online bookshop = Amazon, fast fashion = ASOS. At the moment there aren't that many more...
- Delivery & Returns – this is a major battleground. Speed, price, and reliability are key. In some industries (fashion and hardware/ironmongery) next-day delivery, free if you order by 9pm is becoming the norm. So to get to those levels you also need to have very good systems that keep errors and costs down: real time stock is a must.
- Products – exclusive products, products that are hard to find all play a part here. BUT so does your selection too – do the editing for the customer.
- Price – in commodities markets, there is still a lot of opportunity in being the cheapest. Just don't forget that you have got to be aware of the delivery costs; your customers will factor those in.

USP eCommerce Business Structure Compatibility

	Customer Service	Knowledge & information	Customer Base	Brand	Delivery & Returns	Products	Price
Online Only	•	•	•	•	•	•	•
Mail Order	•	•	•	•	•	•	•
Big Bricks & Clicks	•	•	•	•	•	•	•
Boutique Bricks & Clicks	•	•			•	•	•
Piggyback						•	•
Niche Piggyback	•			•		•	•
Full Multi-channel	•	•	•	•	•	•	•

Your USP also needs to be available – or if it isn't you have got to be able to do it better than the company currently occupying that space. Successful differentiation online becomes a competitive game; once you have successfully differentiated your business, expect the competition to follow. You can never rest and believe you have already got it sorted out. And it's really not easy; it's hard work, it takes time, and it's not cheap. But when you succeed you'll reap the rewards.

Step 1 Complete: What next?

Identifying your eCommerce Business Structure, Product Scope, and USP has shown you what sort of eCommerce business you are going to build. Now you understand that we can start building the three Core Foundations of your eCommerce MasterPlan:

- Step 2 = Core Foundation 1, your Website
- Step 3 = Core Foundation 2, the big numbers: Cost, Profit, and Growth
- Step 4 = Core Foundation 3, products and promotions

As we build your eCommerce MasterPlan, keep asking yourself whenever there's an important decision to be made:

"Does this fit with my eCommerce Business Structure?"
"Does this change my Product Range Scope?"
"Does this help build my USP?"

NOTES

What are the key points from this section?

My eCommerce Business Structure is:

My Product Range Scope is:

My USP is:

Other Notes:

Visit **eCommerceMasterPlan.com** for more information and case studies of businesses with different eCommerce Business Structures, Product Range Scopes, and USPs.

Case Study: Bravissimo

In 1995, Sarah Tremellen set up Bravissimo. Bravissimo started with (and still has) a very niche product range: bras in cup sizes D–KK. So they are very much at the 'niche' end of the product range scale, and they really edit their range to make sure that every product they sell is up to standard. The business started mail order, and has now diversified online and into 21 stores around the UK. It fits perfectly into our MultiChannel eCommerce Business Structure, and is one firm that has done a good job of integrating the three sales channels. When a customer gets to the till in-store, they are asked for their postcode and their customer records are bought up on the till, so the company has a complete view of that customer's interactions with them. Plus, if the item the customer wants isn't in store it can be posted to them, and customers can ask the call centre to deliver to the store for them as well. So the customer sees a VERY joined up process.

In 1995, ladies needing these larger cup sizes would enter their local department store lingerie section and ask, "Do you have anything in my size?", buying what (if anything) was available. Sarah Tremellen's aim was to make it easier for these ladies to find bras that fit, and to have a range of bras to choose from. With her target customers having such a bad experience in the past it would have been easy to just assume that providing the products would be enough to secure the sales. That hasn't been the Bravissimo approach, though. Their USP isn't the larger bra sizes, it's the customer service: every store has a number of well-proportioned changing rooms, each with a chair and pretty gown, plus several fully trained bra fitters, who are able to make sure you have got the right size of bra (which can even fix back problems, and makes you look 10 times better) and know the whole range inside out – even which brand will suit your shape the best. The in-store experience, together with the product selection and joined-up IT systems, show how Bravissimo has put customer service at the centre of everything they do. It's also enabled them to successfully extend the product range from just underwear into swimwear and, most recently, the spin out clothing label PepperBerry.

Case Study: Classic Sailing

Classic Sailing was founded in 1995 by Adam & Debbie Purser, to "take people to sea for safe sailing adventures". It has a very niche range of products: sailing courses and one-to-many-night trips as part of the crew of various sailing ships that voyage around the UK and around the world, everywhere from St Mawes, Cornwall to the Antarctic.

This is a business with a very niche product range, and a fairly niche customer base, too. The business is primarily online, with one mailing per year, so it fits into our Online Only eCommerce Business Structure. The prospective customer base for sailing holidays and courses that Classic Sailing offer is relatively small, so customer retention is essential. The Number One reason someone will book again is because they enjoyed the experience last time, so strong customer service is really important. But it's not the USP.

Classic Sailing's USP is next to impossible for any of their competition to copy, and is founded on Adam and Debbie's love of sailing. Even taking a quick look over their website you can't fail to notice the vast amount of content, and the detail of that content. There's almost the full history of each of their sailing vessels, and full guides to the schedules of each boat, and each specialist trip. Plus blog content on every sailing trip the owners go on themselves, and on those the customers go on, too. If you love sailing, it's a site you can easily lose a Friday afternoon to. This knowledge and information has a multituce of benefits: it brings customers back to the site again and again, it builds the Classic Sailing brand, it attracts new customers in, and it's brilliant for marketing.

Step 2: The First Core Foundation: How to build the right website

eCommerce is all about selling products online. Your website is responsible for displaying your products, getting the visitors to add those products to the basket, and also making sure they order. If your website doesn't do its job, everything else in your business will be more difficult. Even if you have got the best products and marketing in the world you are not going to sell very much if your website isn't pulling its weight.

The website, therefore, is the first of the three Core Foundations of the eCommerce MasterPlan that we're going to tackle.

For two of the eCommerce Business Structures it's not a case of building a website, rather choosing a website to represent them. But choosing the website is still critical for the PiggyBackers, and over the lifetime of the business they may well end up building a site at some point. There are sections in this Step that deal purely with the needs of the PiggyBackers and the non-PiggyBackers, but I would recommend you read all sections at some point, as both sections contain information useful to every eCommerce business.

What does the website need to do?

An eCommerce website is hard to get right because it has to do so many things, and the list increases all the time:

- Showcase your products
- Create/represent your brand (for those only transacting online this is the only place your brand exists)
- Support your marketing activity
- Convert well – that is, get people to buy
- Capture customer information
- Deliver great customer service
- Meet the legal criteria for selling online

It's a real juggling act to get this right. Building and getting a site live usually takes at least three months, sometimes over a year, and the costs can be huge – both what you must pay for the site and the impact that not having it has on sales (time is money, after all). The website is the hardest of the three Core Foundations to fix if it goes wrong.

Products can't be changed very quickly, but they do have a cash value; you are normally going to be able to recover some money from the products that aren't working. Your promotions can be changed in a matter of minutes, so if things aren't working it is easy to change the promotions to make sure the sales are coming in. Marketing is infinitely changeable, and should be altering frequently as new opportunities present themselves. The Website (or, for PiggyBackers, your choice of website) has no intrinsic value, and is very time-consuming and expensive to change, so you need to get it right first time.

In the month before writing this section, I have spoken to five different businesses (not all eCommerce) that are currently battling to get the site they want. All still have a live website that they first started trying to replace 12 months ago, and all are on at least their second website builder. By taking on the advice in the rest of this section you should be able to avoid such a scenario.

Since 2004 I have been involved in project managing over 20 website builds and redesigns on over 10 different software platforms. Budgets ranged from £2,000 to £150,000, and I dealt with stakeholders who knew exactly what they wanted and those who wanted assistance; and not all the projects went smoothly or ended well. There are some things that are common across every product I have been involved in, or heard about, and before we go through how to get the website right first time I'm going to run through what you can expect from a successful build process (yes, all of this will be present in the perfect site build).

You will fall out

At some point in the project, you will fall out with your website builder. It might not be a screaming match, but there will be a point during the build or sign-off phase that you seriously consider sacking the website builders.

It's natural: it's a massive project, it's really complex, you have a massive amount invested in the process, and it's a scary process. It's a process that will take months, and it's not until the site gets delivered that you find out if it was worth it. Of course you are going to fall out with them, or get disappointed. If the whole thing goes smoothly, 100% of the way through, then you have not pushed hard enough to get the site you want.

The last week before the site goes live will be crazy

There will be so much to it, so many pages to proof, so much content to upload and check, endless testing of checkout functionality. You will wonder what you did before the website build project started.

When the site finally goes live you'll want to hug/send a bottle of champagne to your site builders

Until a website is finished and live it's hard to see how it's really going to work (one of the reasons you will fall out). In the last few days it will suddenly come together, and once the site is live you'll finally realise the benefits the site has brought you – sales will go up, the stock will finally be integrated, you won't be printing orders off any more. At this point you will be just a little bit in love with your website builder, and very, very relieved.

In site builds you'll also come across other common issues; time-scales will stretch and there will be nothing you can do about it (never announce the live date to the press until the day it happens). Something that's not in the brief will become critical to your business: you need video, Google's changed its algorithm, you have bought a range of products with the wrong sizing...

I strongly advise anyone who's about to build a website, or has just finished one – actually anyone in eCommerce - to read *Boo Hoo* by Ernst Malmsten[1]. It's the story of boo.com from inception to crash, just 18 months in which they burnt through $135 million. Although all of it happened in 2000, so many of the tales in the book will make anyone involved in a website build giggle and/or roll their eyes.

WORKBOOK
You can download various useful tools for planning and managing a website build from **eCommerceMasterPlan.com/Free**.
Including a Workbook for this section.

---

[1] On the website eCommerceMasterPlan.com you'll find a list of really useful books for eCommerce people including a link to *Boo Hoo*.

How to Get Your Site Build Right First Time

Hopefully the last few paragraphs haven't scared you off building an eCommerce website. The key to a successful build lies in the planning. This is also the key to getting value for money – only having the functionality you need. Most builds that fail do so because either:

- The in-house stakeholders aren't in agreement, so the scope changes
- The brief wasn't detailed enough
- What the merchant wrote and what the website builder read in the brief was understood in different ways: you said "Zoom" and meant bigger-picture-in-a-pop-up; they heard "Zoom" and thought interactive zoom to the level of Google Maps.

Thus, the majority of the failures are built in at the start of the project, which means you can easily build them out of the project.

- Prepare the Brief

The brief is the document you are going to send out to the companies who are going to tender for the job of building your website. Even if you are just upgrading the site you have got and sticking with the same website builder, you should still create a fool-proof brief. The brief enables you to make sure everything your company needs is going to be provided. It will also give you the opportunity to get all your internal stakeholders to agree on what the website's going to do. If you get the brief right, everything else is going to go smoothly.

Be aware, however, that the brief will change between you sending it to the website builders and when you sign on the dotted line and the project actually kicks off. That's because your website builders will have ideas about how the site in your brief can be improved further; things you thought would be out of the price range won't be, and other things it will be possible to do better. Finally, there may be one item you have included that's not critical and adds substantially to either time-scales or cost. These changes you need to feed back to your stakeholders to make sure everyone's happy.

Stakeholders

These are the people around the business (or in a small organisation the different hats you yourself wear) who have different needs from the website. Broadly they are:

- Product Team (buyers and merchandising) – get them involved so you know what the products are and how you need to sell them. Do the products have different sizing? Colours? And what information needs to be displayed with each product?
- Online merchandisers – what do they need to be able to do with the Content Management System?
- Customer Services – find out what key problems the customers have; how can the new site fix these (FAQs, how to build it videos, call us/email us buttons)
- IT/Warehouse – integration. Critical to get this right as it can save hours and money. Find out what integration they need, and how best to do it.
- Finance – what payment methods are you using/can you use?

- Marketing – what feeds and tracking do they need? What is required for SEO (Search Engine Optimisation), for Social media? What promotions do the website need to be able to run?
- Brand – what should the site look like?
- The owner.

In your business there may be more stakeholders than this, so take half an hour to consider who needs to be involved and why.

There are a lot of areas of input into a website for an eCommerce business; it's important to get them all understood early in the process because the success of the business depends on getting it all right.

1. The Brief

Once you have the input of all the stakeholders, you may find conflict between them about what they all want that you will have to resolve before putting the site out to tender.

Make the brief really detailed; if it's less than five pages you have not got enough information in it. And you may want to include mock-ups of how it might look, as well as an example set of product data. The more detail you put in, the more effective the tendering process will be, and the smoother the website build project, too.

Once you are happy with the brief, get each stakeholder to check it over too: if you get them to all agree at this point it makes the rest of the process much more straightforward. At this point, also explain to them what their involvement from here on in will be. You need to manage their expectations and their involvement – what will you need them to sign off at the end of the project, if anything?

As well as all the detailed information, it is worth putting in some background colour to the project: why do you want the new site, what are your hopes for it? Plus an estimate of site traffic volumes – hosting is expensive, and a slow site will kill your sales.

2. The Tender Process

Once the whole company is happy with the brief, it can be sent to the website builders. If you are running a full tender process then pick 3–5 different builders, but make sure each would be able to do the job for you; an exploratory phone call before including them can save you a lot of time.

Each builder will come back to you in a different way. That's OK. The structure they come back with enables them to fit their technology to your needs in the easiest way for them. You want them to do a good job if you pick them, so making it easy for them to do the job will save you time and money and reduce errors. Letting them respond in their own style also gives you an insight into how they work, and that's a great thing to find out, too.

In addition to what they send back, you are going to want to meet with them. Critical things to include in the meeting are:

- Question anything that doesn't make sense to you in their response. This is your opportunity to really understand what they can/can't do for you.
- Have a live run-through of their back end system – you want to understand how easy the CMS is to use, and how much functionality it gives you. Explore everything: this is often the stage at which you find out a few bits that don't meet your expectation.
- Explore the front end. How much can you change? How much is totally set in stone?
- You might also want them to provide some artworked mock-ups to prove they understand your brand.
- Ask about time scales: when can they fit in your build, how busy are they right now?
- How much stretch have they put into the project? What happens is the scope of costs and timescales grows beyond this?

It will be a long meeting. Don't forget to make sure your systems team are happy with the integration plans.

Once you have had the meeting and you have got their prices, you need to speak to some people they have already built sites for and road-test their websites. Key questions to ask them are:

- Was the project on time?
- Was the project on budget?
- How were they to work with?
- How have the support and costs been since the site went live?

The last question is possibly the most important. If the site build goes well you could be working with the company for years. You need to understand how they are to work with post-live.

– Pricing Structures

Never only buy a website based on the build price. Website pricing is more complicated than that. There will always be follow-on costs, hosting, software license fees, maintenance, and support retainers. You need to factor in what these are, and fully understand what it is and isn't covered in the overall price.

– Signing and Kicking Off

Once you are happy you have found the right website builder, you are going to need to sign some sort of contract with them. This is also a great opportunity to finalise exactly what's in the brief. It won't be the same one that you sent to them in the beginning; you'll have learnt things you want to include during the tender process, and they will have pulled the brief into their format. So take the time to make sure all of you are 100% agreed on the final scope.

3. The Build

The first thing you want to agree on once the build is underway are the timescales. When is everything required? When are members of your team going to need to be ready to sign off? And how much movement is there in the plan?

Put all the important dates in your diary – and in the diary of anyone else who needs to contribute.

Keep referring back to the brief. Try not to go beyond it and, if the builders are not following it, bring them back on track as soon as possible.

Most website builders will tell you they have a project manager who will oversee everything for you. I have never worked with one who does. I have worked with many great website-builder-side project managers, but, however good they are, they are not a member of your team, they are a member of the website builder's team. They don't understand what you are trying to achieve as well as you do, and they are highly unlikely to invest time motivating your team to provide things on time and correctly. So you need to manage the project, too.

As soon as you are underway, convert the brief/to do list into whatever format you need it in to make sure everything happens and happens right; be that a mind map, a project planning tool, an Excel spreadsheet, a Google doc, or a very large white board, get it right and explain to the key people how it's to be used (especially the website-builder-side project manager). If you do it really successfully, it will become your key method of communication with the website builders – the foundation of every call and meeting agenda.

DOWNLOAD...
There's an example website project planner available on the website at **eCommerceMasterPlan.com/Free**.

4. Putting the new site live

The first rule of putting the new website live is to make sure you are 100% happy with it. Test everything again and again and again. For most site builders, the point when the website goes live marks the end of the build phase – so any changes after that are chargeable.

It is always tempting to go live with a few things outstanding in order to hit the deadline, but be very careful if you do because you might be stuck with a very large bill.

A few days before the site goes live, make sure you have got access to the DNS hosting for your domain (HYPERLINK "http://www.yourwebsite.com/" www.yourwebsite.com). Then change the TTL to a few minutes or seconds; the TTL is the Time to Live – that is how often your domain records are refreshed, so if it's set to 24 hours it will take a long time for your new website to go live. Then at the appointed time change, the A record is to point to the new hosting IP address.

Once you have made that change, there are a few things you need to do, almost immediately.

The first is to check the site is working. Place a few orders, do some navigating, sign up for emails, etc. Make sure it's all working on the front end, but also that any data submitted is ending up where it should (orders to the warehouse, email sign-ups to your database, etc.).

Once you are happy, let the rest of the business know it's changed over. Be ready to deal with "but I can still see the old site", and have IT refresh the office cache and individuals' PC caches. It is probably best to explain to everyone that DNS propagation can take a while as all the name-servers around the internet are updated with your new hosting location; this can take a couple of days. An annoying headache, and it is always either the most PC-incompetent person in the office, or the boss whose computer is the last to see the new website.

Next you need to check and set up the non-critical functionality of the new website (that's the stuff that the customers won't have noticed). Is all your tracking code working –analytics and reporting, etc.? At this point you also want to make sure Google Base (etc.) is picking up on new feeds.

Finally, monitor the performance and tweak what you need to; a website is never finished.

Selecting the right PiggyBack Site

Unlike getting the build of your own site wrong, it's not that financially expensive if you get the choice of PiggyBack site wrong, although you will still lose all the time you have spent getting your account set up, your shop sorted out, and your products listed – so it's worth trying to make the right decision first time.

The other big difference is that you can use multiple PiggyBack sites; you are not restricted to just the one website.

> **WORKBOOK**
> You can download a workbook for this section from
> **eCommerceMasterPlan.com/Free.**

Why Use more than one PiggyBack Website?

If you are a normal PiggyBacker then you are pretty much limited to two options of website to PiggyBack on: Amazon and eBay. You will most likely end up on both of them because that's how you maximize your sales. Both attract a mainstream audience but there are lots of people who only use one of these, so you are missing out on sales if you only use one.

For the Niche PiggyBacker there are hundreds of choices, and they are often difficult to compare until you have tried them out. Each also taps into a slightly different market; some are international, some just for one country, so you want to test out one or two to make sure you find the place that will sell your products the fastest and the most profitably.

Put simply, you should use more than one PiggyBack site in order to get your products in front of multiple audiences and increase your sales.

How to Choose your PiggyBack Websites

The decision will be based on three areas:

- Financial – how much does it cost you to put your products on the website? What i's the model of charges? This varies from a monthly subscription to a simple commission – and everything in between.
- Systems – can you integrate with your own systems? How easy is it to upload products? How easy is it to process orders and deal with queries? How helpful and accessible are the PiggyBack sites when you need them?
- Marketing – What's the PiggyBack site's customer base? How well do they market you? What help do they provide? How easy is it to customise your 'shop'?

The importance of these three areas will depend on your needs and the strategy of your business. If you are a designer selling a few really attractive products, then 'shop' customisation and how the products look is going to be more important than pricing or systems. If you are selling in your spare time and don't like technology very much, then systems and the fees structure is going to be really key; you don't want to be paying a subscription in months when you have nothing for sale. If you are interested in selling lots of products, systems and marketing are going to be key.

The very first thing you need to do is find out what options there are in your marketplace. You can do this by simply searching on Google for products like yours and seeing where they are being sold. It's also a good idea to tap into some industry knowledge: get on the forums frequented by businesses selling similar products and find out where they sell.

Once you have got the list, start by simply looking at each of the sites and ask yourself if it's somewhere you would be happy for your products to be promoted. If it's not, take it off the list. Although this is rather subjective it's important to be on websites that enhance your brand, and where people would expect to find your products.

Next you need to work through the following checklist so that you can compare your options. The checklist is split into three areas: Financial, Systems, and Marketing.

DOWNLOAD...
On the website (at **eCommerceMasterPlan.com/Free**) we have created a directory of PiggyBack websites, so have a look to see what's in your marketplace.

Financial Criteria

- Is there a set-up cost? What is it?
- Is there a subscription fee (a fee you must pay every year/month/day whether you sell or not)? How much is it?
- Are there listing fees (a fee for each item you list)? How much?
- Is there a commission on your sales? How much?
- How does postage charging work?
- What's the payment method? Do they take the money and pass it on to you, or do you need to take the money yourself – through a PayPal account, for example?
- How do you get paid? How soon do you get the money? If you are using your own PayPal account it will be almost instant, but if they are taking the money, how long will it be before you get paid?

Once you have the answers to all these questions you will need to model what the charges on each are going to add up to for your business. So estimate a month's sales and calculate how much it's going to cost you in fees. Don't forget to work out how much postage will cost. Then you have got a price per month that allows you to compare the sites.

Systems Criteria

The Systems Criteria checklist will be different for each business, so if one of these is irrelevant for you, leave it out.

- Can you integrate with your own systems? If you have an existing product system or order-taking system can you integrate it all? How easy is it? How much will that cost?
- How easy is to upload products? Can you use a spreadsheet to bulk upload, or does each need to be done separately?
- How many images can you upload for each item?
- Can you upload video or audio for the products?
- How easy is it to process orders and deal with queries? Do they have a communication centre you can use for this, or do you have to manage it via your own email account?
- How helpful and accessible are the PiggyBack site when you need them? Do you get a phone number to call, or is it just a help centre?

This set of criteria isn't as easy to compare as the Financial Criteria, so give each website a mark out of five in each area for how well they meet what you need, and then total them up.

Marketing Criteria

- Who is the customer base? Does it fit with your target customers?
- How busy is their site? You really want a number of visitors, rather than hits of page views.
- How well do their customers buy? What's the conversion rate?
- In what ways will they promote you? Emails? Search advertising? Features on the website or blog?
- Can you customise your shop?
- What help do they give you to increase your sales? Webinars, training, advice? (Etsy is great at this.)

- How well SEOed will your product pages be? Can you affect this?
- Do they have Social Sharing buttons on the product pages?
- Do they have a customer review or comments system?
- Do they feed into Google Base?
- Is there an option to buy extra promotion on the site?
- How good is their on-site search engine? Try a few searches and see if you get relevant results.
- Can you cross-sell your products?
- What promotions can you run?

Some of these marketing elements might not seem immediately important right now, but once you have read the following sections on the marketing activity for eCommerce, you will be glad you checked them out.

Once all the data is gathered it should be easy to whittle down your list to the top two or three you are going to try out. Don't start them all at once. Pick the best option and start building that first, get your account set up, get your shop ready, set up your products, and deal with at least a few weeks' worth of orders – and make changes as you go. Once you are happy that you have got that site working well for you, then – and only then – move on to site number two. If you try to do all of them at once you risk getting confused and it taking forever to get each working for you.

As you use the PiggyBack sites, you'll find that different products work well on different sites – so focus your effort on those. You may find one site doesn't work for you, or stops working for you; don't be afraid to pull out, or at least cut back the product range you have there.

Your Website's Most Important Job

Whatever type of site you need, remember that a good eCommerce website must:

- Convert traffic to sales
- Represent your brand well
- Attract customers

The most important of these is to convert the traffic to sales. If your website doesn't convert the traffic to sales easily, then everything else you do will be less effective than it should be.

Consider the simple equation:

Traffic x Average Order Value (AOV) x Conversion Rate = Sales

If each month you get 1,000 people to your website, and your average order value is £50, consider the impact of a stronger conversation rate:
A poorly converting website:

- Traffic = 1,000
- AOV = £50
- Conversion Rate = 1.5%

　　1,000 x £50 x 1.5% = £750

If the website converts just a little better:

- Traffic = 1,000
- AOV = £50
- Conversion Rate = 2.5%

1,000 x £50 x 2.5% = £1,250

That's a 60% sales increase. It's not difficult to get a website to convert at 2.5%, but many don't. A well put-together website will also help increase your AOV.

To ensure your website does its job properly, you need to remove as many barriers to conversion as possible. A barrier to conversion is anything that stops the customer from buying from you. Most are based on confusion, uncertainty, or distraction. If a customer is confused they won't buy, if a customer is uncertain that what you are selling is what they want they won't buy, and if they get distracted they'll forget to buy.

Tackling Barriers to Conversion

The first step is to find those barriers. To do this you need to look at the website stats: where are people leaving your conversion funnel, where do they exit the site from? What products are most often put in the basket but not bought? Then look at your website, go through it from end to end, and look out for areas of uncertainty, potential confusion, and distractions.

Common Barriers to Conversion

- Navigation in the checkout – take a look at Amazon's checkout; once you are in the basket there's nothing you can do but proceed with your order.
- Buttons – are your buying buttons easy to follow? Do you always put the one to proceed in the same place and in the same colour? Are the words on the buttons clear and do they promote an action? "Buy now" will work better than "Buy".
- Hidden Postage – make sure your customer is aware of postage options early on, as soon as they get to the website. Lots of people will drop out if they get to the checkout and suddenly get hit with a £5 charge they weren't expecting.
- Delivery speeds – be upfront about these too. When people buy, they want to know when they are going to receive their order.
- Contact Details – don't hide them. Let people know how to call or email you, and explain how fast you'll get back to them if they do. They may well not call, but if they know they can then that reduces their uncertainty and increases their trust in you. Your address is important, too.
- Product information – after delivery, this is the major cause of confusion and uncertainty. Include the information the customer needs. Sizes, dimensions, and some compelling written copy are really key.
- Product Photos – if the dress is available in blue, the customer needs to see the whole dress in blue – not just a swatch of that colour.
- Promotions – make 'em simple. Really simple. If there's anything complex then keep explaining what the customer needs to do.

Plus there is one thing you can do to improve conversion across the board, and reduce the impact of customer confusion, uncertainty, and distraction: that is to prove that customers can trust you. If they trust you and like you, they are going to persist a little more to make that purchase, they are less likely to be confused, they trust that the areas they are uncertain about will be OK, and if not they know you will honour a refund. A customer who trusts you is far more likely to remember to come back post-distraction and make the purchase.

If your chosen USP is Customer Service, then you have pretty much got that wrapped up; likewise if you have a strong brand or strong customer base. Whatever your relationship with your customers, there are a few things you can do to the website to help build that trust.

- Add security logos to the site – the credit cards you accept, whichever service you are using to secure your payment area – Sagepay or Verisign. These increase customer trust.
- Have a proper privacy policy and terms and conditions – and don't hide them. Writing them so they can be read easily is also helpful.
- Fix anything that's broken.
- Have a clear and easy-to-find and read returns policy.
- Think about adding a guarantee.
- Have an 'About Us' page; show who you are. And include your company history.
- Awards help, too, as do the ISIS and IDIS logos managed by the IMRG (see IMRG.org).

> **WEBSITE**
> You'll find more ideas for improving conversion, and building a better website on the website: **eCommerceMasterPlan.com**

Step 2 Complete: What next?

Your eCommerce website is at the centre of your business. If it doesn't work, your business will fail. Invest as much time and money as you can into getting it right, but invest wisely. On day one, an eCommerce business can do very well on a site that only costs a few thousand pounds, but if you are a bigger business your site must live up to customer expectations.

A website can take a few months to build and get live; whilst that's being built you need to be working on the other two Core Foundations.

- Step 2 = Core Foundation 1, your website ✔
- Step 3 = Core Foundation 2, the big numbers
- Step 4 = Core Foundation 3, products and promotions

NOTES

What are the key points from this section?

Traffic x Average Order Value x Conversion Rate = Success

Top Tip: Often-overlooked Points to Put in your Website Brief

Some of these add clarity to what you would normally put, others are little extras it's worth getting added in.

- Google Base Feed
- RSS feed for the blog
- Full Google Analytics tracking – including search and ecommerce
- A checkout with conversion funnel reporting
- URL structure for SEO
- Auto-generating metadata for SEO
- Outline all the promotions you are going to want to run
- Which address look-up service do you want to use?
- Outline how you will categorise your products, and the data you have to display for them
- Include which browser/operating system configurations you want the site to work on (we've a list of the current ones to include on the website **eCommerceMasterPlan.com/Free**)

Step 3: The Second Core Foundation: Cost, profit, and growth

In the last Step, we looked at the key sales equation for an eCommerce business:

$$\text{Traffic} \times \text{AOV} \times \text{Conversion Rate} = \text{Sales}$$

Unfortunately eCommerce isn't quite that simple; you can't survive on sales alone. You need to be making a profit. The good news is that a successful eCommerce business builds profit into their model from day one by setting the right margin level to work at (the margin is the difference between what you buy the product for and what you sell it for).

Plus, in eCommerce, it's pretty easy to then use an ROI (return on investment) calculation to properly analyse the business and make sure you are always optimising it. Put simply, optimisation is the process of deciding what to keep doing, what to stop doing, and what to work harder at.

So before you can dive in to products, promotions, and marketing, you need to make sure you have got a firm grip on the financials of your business, so that you can be certain your efforts will lead to profit.

WORKBOOK
A workbook to help you identify these ways for making profit for your business is downloadable from the website **eCommerceMasterPlan.com/Free**

Margin – the Foundation of your future Profit

At the heart of any eCommerce business success lies the Margin. The margin is the difference between the price you pay for your stock, and the amount for which you sell it to your customers. It is quite easy to identify your margin, but it's much harder to work out what it should be – and to keep it there.

THE MARGIN

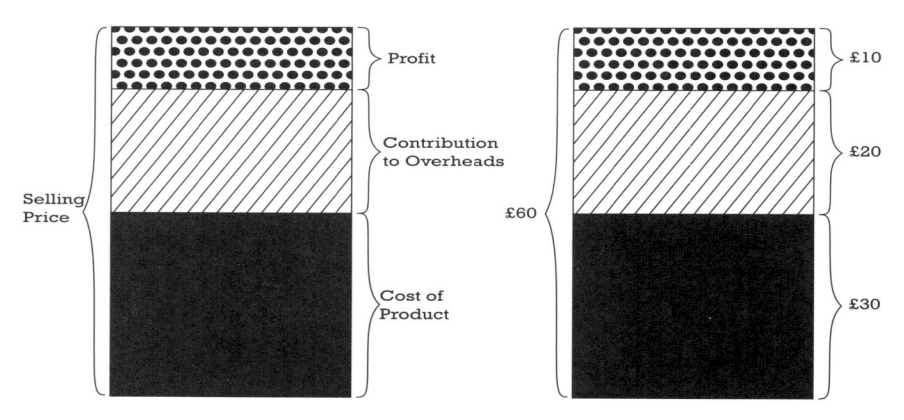

Diagram: Selling Price broken into Profit, Contribution to Overheads, and Cost of Product. Second example: £10 Profit, £20 Contribution to Overheads, £30 Cost of Product, totalling £60.

The margin is what enables you to cover all your overheads (warehousing, website, staff, power, etc.). Every product you sell needs to contribute to the overhead costs, hence in many businesses reference is made to "contribution" rather than "profit". Once all those bills are paid, whatever you are left with is your profit.

MARGIN AND CONTRIBUTION

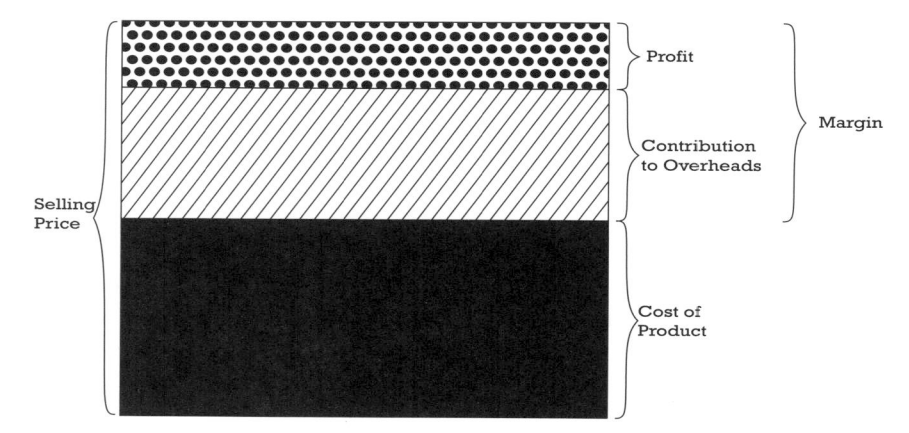

Diagram: Selling Price broken into Profit, Contribution to Overheads, and Cost of Product. Margin = Profit + Contribution to Overheads.

So, it's critical to get your margin on every product right or you won't make any money, or – even worse – you won't be able to cover your overheads.

Return on Investment (ROI): Making sure you are on track

Return on Investment (ROI) is the number which enables you to see how well you are doing (so long as it's positive!). Return on Investment is the profit (Return) on what you have spent (Investment): it's usually presented as a percentage. At a business level you will calculate it as follows:

ROI = (PROFIT) DIVIDED BY TOTAL COSTS

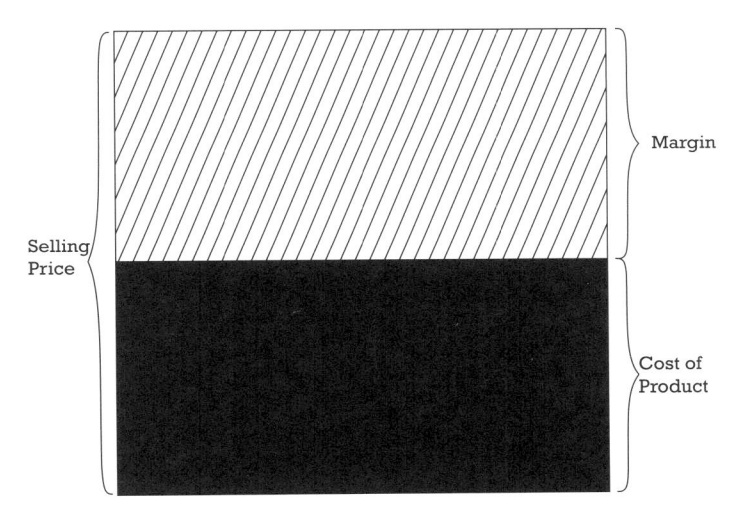

[Diagram: A rectangle representing Selling Price, divided into two parts. The upper hatched portion is labelled "Margin", and the lower solid black portion is labelled "Cost of Product".]

ROI = 10 divided by (20 plus 30)
ROI = 10 divided by 50
ROI = 20%

This ROI enables you to compare performance – this year vs last year, this month vs last month, and see how well your business is doing. As you can see, the margin very much underpins this, which is why it's really important to understand what your margin is AND what it needs to be to hit the desired ROI.

Once you have a handle on your business' ROI, you can then create a working ROI which you can use to measure the marketing performance or product performance. This needs to be an ROI you can quickly use on any marketing spend and return figures, otherwise you have got to work out all your costs and then apportion them to each traffic driving channel before you can see what is and isn't working. Instead you want to be working with a very simple ROI:

Marketing ROI = (Sales – Marketing cost) divided by (Marketing Cost)

This gives you a rough ROI, which ignores product costs and overheads but will, as overheads are fixed, enable you to easily measure what's working best. So let's take an example:

MARKETING CHANNEL PERFORMANCE: MAY 2012

Channel	Orders	Sales	Cost
Email	100	£5,000.00	£2,000.00
PPC	60	£2,400.00	£2,000.00
eBay	150	£4,500.00	£500.00

Taking these numbers, our email ROI will be:

Email ROI = Profit divided by Cost
Email ROI = (Sales – Cost) divided by Cost
Email ROI = (5,000 – 2,000) divided by 2,000
Email ROI = 150%

Using the same method, we can work out the ROI for the other channels, too:

MARKETING CHANNEL ROI

Channel	Orders	Sales	Cost	ROI
Email	100	£5,000.00	£2,000.00	150.00%
PPC	60	£2,400.00	£2,000.00	20.00%
eBay	150	£4,500.00	£500.00	800.00%

From these results we can now see that even though email drives the most sales, the eBay channel is the most profitable.

Alternatively, if you don't like percentages, you can use a **Cost/Profit per order** metric:

Cost/Profit per Order = (Sales – Marketing Cost) divided by (number of orders)

So, our example about this would give us:

Email Cost/Profit per Order = (5,000 – 2,000) divided by 100
Email Cost/Profit per Order = (3,000) divided by 100
Email Cost/Profit per Order = £30 profit per order

MARKETING CHANNEL COST/PROFIT PER ORDER

Channel	Orders	Sales	Cost	ROI	C/P per Order
Email	100	£5,000.00	£2,000.00	150.00%	£30.00
PPC	60	£2,400.00	£2,000.00	20.00%	£6.66
eBay	150	£4,500.00	£500.00	800.00%	£26.66

As you can see above, it's quite useful to work out this metric as well as ROI, because here we can see that our email customers are worth more to us than our eBay customers.

So, if you know you can afford to spend £20 on recruiting a new customer, and your marketing channels show a Cost/Profit per Order of -£15, then everything is on track. You can use the same theory to look at the ROI of different products, different promotions, or even different time periods.

Scale

Whether you find Cost/Profit per Order or ROI easier to use, for either to yield results you need a certain scale of orders, because you have overheads to cover and products sat on the shelves.

Your overheads for the year are basically fixed, so you need to generate a certain volume of orders to cover them. For example:

Overheads = £100,000
Margin per order = £20

Orders to cover overheads = 5,000

So (assuming the margin holds and the overheads come in on budget) in this example you would need to generate 5,000 orders to break even. It will only be from the 5,001st order that you see a profit.

Analytics – the numbers that are going to keep everything on track

In eCommerce we are bombarded with metrics. It's numbers, numbers, numbers – everywhere. So the challenge can often be to work out which numbers to focus on. By identifying your KPIs and using the tools we've run through, you have taken a big step in the right direction.

What we also need to make sure is that the numbers we're looking at are accurate. And that means making sure your systems are giving you the right numbers (although we're not going to go into it here, that includes the information you are getting from your accountants and from your order processing systems).

The first thing to get set up properly is your website analytics. Google Analytics is a free package that can be set up very easily and that will give you most of what you need to understand your website and marketing performance. There are other analytics tools available. Whichever you choose, make sure they are correctly in place, with:

- every page tagged accurately
- conversion tracking accurately implemented on the order confirmation page, and turned on in Google Analytics.

You'll also find that a lot of your marketing tools have their own conversion tracking that can be implemented; most email marketing systems will have some code to be added to the order confirmation page, as do Google Adwords and Microsoft Adcentre in PPC. You will often find that it's necessary to set these tracking systems up as well, because when you get the conversion data fed back into those tools, it makes it easier to analyse how well they are working. For example, setting up the Google Adwords Conversion Tracking will show you the orders driven by each keyword and adtext – essential for the optimisation process.

So don't be afraid to set up all the conversion tracking options you have got (it's also very useful for when one of them has a bad day!). Before you start setting them up, though, be clear on what you want the value to be. Most conversion tracking codes allow a real number to be put into the value field (so you'll know if the order was for £5 or £500 – very important!). You need to decide what this number is going to be.

- Including or excluding VAT?
- Including or excluding Postage?
- Don't forget to check your website can handle this!

I would always advise tracking it exc. postage, but inc./exc. VAT depends on your business and how you usually look at the numbers. Whichever value format you choose, make sure that it's set up in the same way for EVERY piece of tracking code you put in place, and that you always use the same number in your analysis.

Setting your eCommerce MasterPlan Objectives

At the beginning of this section, we looked at the basic business objectives:

- your target ROI (or Cost/Profit per Order): the Profit
- the number of orders you need to cover the overheads: the Scale

Neither of these is going to be your only objective for the next 12 months. You don't want to only cover your overheads (which your Scale objective will do); you need to sell more than that to have a profit you can use to invest in the business for growth in the years to come.

The analysis you have done so far will have given you some pointers into what your objectives for the year might be, but here are some further commonly used objectives for eCommerce businesses:

- Average Order Value (AOV) – a great way to increase profitability because you are going to cover more overhead costs with each order, but going for a high AOV can reduce response.
- Conversion Rate – increasing customer response from your marketing is a great way to increase turn over. The more orders you get from each £100 of marketing spend the better!
- Traffic Volumes – if you know your website converts well, then focusing on the traffic you can get to the website makes a lot of sense.
- Sales Value – every company should have sales targets!

- Number of Orders – if you need to acquire customers in the next 12 months then this is worth focusing on
- Conversion to Website Buyer – how many of your customers can you get to order online rather than via other channels? If customers ordering online is best for your business (cheaper etc.), then this can be a useful objective.

It will lead to confusion and you missing targets if you try to aim for all of these objectives, so you need to choose two or three to be your KPIs (Key Performance Indicators) for the year – the ones you check at least monthly. And there should be at least one KPI for scale and one for ROI (profitability).

Working out the Marketing Budget for the Coming Year: Gap analysis

Now you have:

- your objectives for the year ahead.

We also need to look at:

- where continuity and natural growth will take you.

Put simply, that's what you achieved last year. (We're going to cover a more complex analysis in Step 5).

This means you can easily see where the gap is between the continuity performance and your objectives. Plus the level you can't afford to go below:

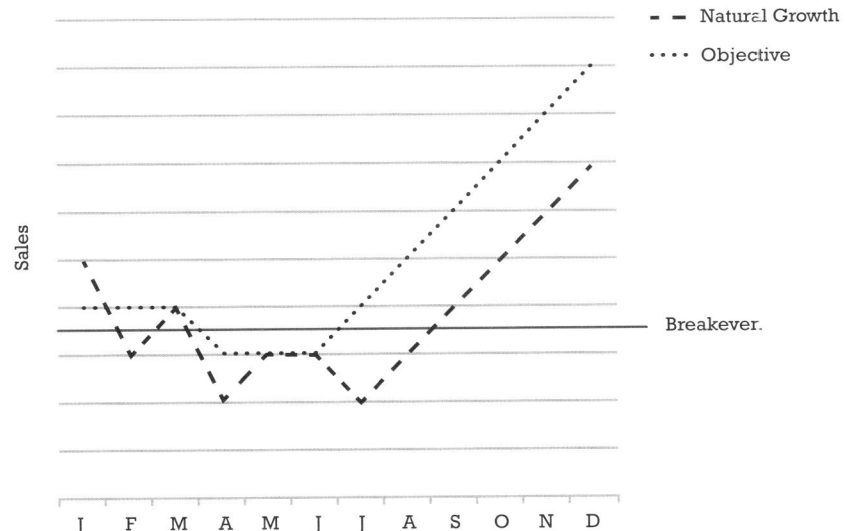

PERFORMANCE, SHOWING GAP TO BE FILLED

Filling that Gap and making sure you stay ahead of your break-even position are the jobs of your Marketing Plan. But you also need enough products to sell!

As you know your margin, you can take those sales totals for each year and work out how much you need to spend on products to have enough to sell.

You also know the ROI you need to achieve – so it's easy to work out how much more you can afford to spend on marketing to make sure you fill the gaps. That, plus the value of last year's marketing spend, is what this year's marketing budget will be.

Step 3 Complete: What next?

This is probably the most difficult step to work through in your eCommerce MasterPlan – so well done for getting this far!

We've now run through the numbers behind successful eCommerce, how to convert them into budgets for your eCommerce MasterPlan, and how to measure your performance in order to keep your plan on target.

To build your successful eCommerce MasterPlan then, you need to understand:

- What your ROI is (or cost/profit per order)
- How many orders you need to generate over the year
- The size of your marketing budget

Now we need to build the activity these numbers enable – the products, the promotions, and the marketing plan.

- Step 2 = Core Foundation 1, your website ✔
- Step 3 = Core Foundation 2, the big numbers ✔
- Step 4 = Core Foundation 3, products and promotions

NOTES

What are the key points from this section?

My Margin is:

My ROI (or Cost/Sales) is:

My Marketing (or working ROI) is:

My Objectives for the next 12 months are:

Other Notes:

Top Tip: The Attribution Debate

The biggest debate in eCommerce performance at the moment is how you should attribute a sale to each channel. During the work-up to an order, one customer may have visited your site many times via several different routes, e.g.:

Magazine Website > email > "red widget" PPC > brand PPC > affiliate > PURCHASE

WEBSITE
Visit **eCommerceMasterPlan.com** for more information.

Which route deserves the credit for the sale?

Traditionally attribution has been done on a 'last click wins' model – so whatever marketing was tracked driving the customer to the website just before the sale gets the sale. But that gives a skewed view of marketing performance; in the above example your PR, email and PPC get no credit.

This also gets very complicated when you take offline activity into account. Imagine the customer also received a catalogue from you, or went into a store: how do you reward the store and the catalogue for their impact on the sale? How do you know they had an impact?

As yet there is no clear route to track the impact of offline marketing, and most companies stick with the imperfect 'last click wins' because it's the easiest to do – it's what Google Analytics automatically does.

If you choose to do that too, be aware that the other tracking codes on your website (the email one, the PPC one) will report complete data, so everyone influenced by an email will be reported back to the email tool. So if you take performance reports direct from those tools you will count some sales twice.

Top Tip: Google Analytics

- If you can get the Google Analytics eCommerce tracking set up fully, then you will also get product sales data, which is REALLY useful for quickly seeing which promotions drove sales of which product.
- Do check that the "This site is an ecommerce site" box is ticked if you are in the process of setting up the tracking! If the box is unticked, it will look as if the tracking isn't working.
- Make sure you have an Admin account; if your login only has "User" access, ask for this to be changed.
- If you are using Google Adwords, link it with your Google Analytics account: it will give you much better reporting on Adwords' performance.
- Consider setting up a goal for successful catalogue requests or email sign-ups.
- You can create custom dashboards, which are really useful for a quick and easy check of what's going on
- You can also set any report to automatically email to a set distribution list each month/day/week – VERY useful for keeping people informed. And for making sure you don't forget to look at the numbers!
- Google have released a very simple tool that lets you easily add tracking code to any link into your website, so if you run a promotion with a magazine, you can tag all the links from the magazine back to you , which means you can easily see the impact of that data.

WEBSITE
You can find a link to this tool at **eCommerceMasterPlan.com/Free**

Top Tip: Costs You Shouldn't Forget

- Utilities (electric, gas, water)
- Rent and business rates
- Warehousing
- Accountants
- Lawyers
- Software licenses
- Salaries and National Insurance
- Packing Materials
- Stationery
- Computers
- Phones
- IT support
- Returns and written-off stock
- Tax – Corporation and VAT

Top Tip: P&P – Profit or Cost?

As late as the 2000s, the mail order industry aimed to make a healthy profit on its postage and packing charges. So, if the customer paid £4.99, the average cost to the merchant was most likely £4, £3, or even less.

Now, it's hard to find a website that doesn't have free P&P over some level of spend – and the level of spend is getting lower year on year. This has been driven by two factors:

Customers react really positively to Free P&P promotions, because a P&P charge is a big blocker to conversion. So why not always have a Free P&P offer?

Businesses whose USP is Customer Service, or Delivery and Returns, or Customer Base all have good reason to keep the P&P low.

We have seen Amazon taking their minimum Free Delivery spend ever lower, and also introducing the concept of a subscription delivery service with Amazon Prime. This is being copied by other ecommerce sites: Ocado have a range of different subscriptions depending on whether you want peak-time or off-peak delivery slots.

At the extreme end is Ironmongery Direct (Customer Service USP), who will deliver a £45 order for free on a Next Day service (so long as you order by 7.30pm). But they are something of an exception, as most companies only offer free delivery on the cheapest delivery service (usually Royal Mail 2nd Class) and charge market rates for faster services.

You need to decide what your P&P structure is going to be. Making the wrong decision on your P&P charges can be expensive. So be careful to balance customer service with your own profitability.

Top Tip: P&P – Profit or Cost?

As late as the 2000s, the mail order industry aimed to make a healthy profit on its postage and packing charges. So, if the customer paid £4.99, the average cost to the merchant was most likely £4, £3, or even less.

Now, it's hard to find a website that doesn't have free P&P over some level of spend – and the level of spend is getting lower year on year. This has been driven by two factors:

- Customers react really positively to Free P&P promotions, because a P&P charge is a big blocker to conversion. So why not always have a Free P&P offer?
- Businesses whose USP is Customer Service, or Delivery and Returns, or Customer Base all have good reason to keep the P&P low.

We have seen Amazon taking their minimum Free Delivery spend ever lower, and also introducing the concept of a subscription delivery service with Amazon Prime. This is being copied by other ecommerce sites: Ocado have a range of different subscriptions depending on whether you want peak-time or off-peak delivery slots.

At the extreme end is Ironmongery Direct (Customer Service USP), who will deliver a £45 order for free on a Next Day service (so long as you order by 7.30pm). But they are something of an exception, as most companies only offer free delivery on the cheapest delivery service (usually Royal Mail 2nd Class) and charge market rates for faster services.

You need to decide what your P&P structure is going to be. Making the wrong decision on your P&P charges can be expensive. So be careful to balance customer service with your own profitability.

Top Tip: Customer Lifetime Value – Taking your business to the next level of profitability

The aims of your marketing plan and your customer segmentation are to find the most effective way to meet your ROI and Volume targets. At the absolute centre of getting this right is knowing that your marketing spend is going in the right places. The customer segmentation exercise will help you work out how you can up AOVs and which customers to focus on, but to really make the whole system sing you need to understand your Customer Lifetime Value (CLV).

CLV is the amount a person will spend with you in their lifetime minus the amount you spent servicing that customer. So it's basically the profit you will get from each customer. It's an amazing number to know for two reasons:

Firstly, if your overall CLV is £100, you know you can spend up to £99 to recruit a customer and you will turn a profit. But not all customers are going to have a positive CLV...

Now, this is where CLV becomes really exciting! Once you are able to work out CLV at customer level, you can plug it into your segmentation model. That enables you to see:

- The profitability of each segment – and some segments won't be profitable. Those segments you should cut back on your marketing to and focus that marketing on moving them into another segment. Get them to order via more channels, more frequently, at a higher AOV, etc.
- How much you can afford to spend to recruit the right types of customer, because you have tracked the source of the data so you can see CLV by data source.
- Which segments you should do MORE marketing to in order to move them into better segments, or to increase their profit even more.

Work out your CLV

In an ideal world, you would be able to divide every cost in the business accurately to each order you process and allocate each order back to a customer. Achieving that will change every process in the business and keep a bevy of analysts in work for months. There is a way to do it more quickly in order to get the benefits faster (and of course you might later choose to make it more complex), so just start with a 12-month CLV:

- Take all your costs for the last 12 months.
- Divide by the number of orders you processed in the last 12 months.
- Now you have your total cost per order (hopefully it is lower than your Average Order Value!).
- Divide the number of orders you had last year by the number of people who bought from you last year: this is your average orders per customer.

- Multiply your average order value by the average orders per customer: this gives you your average spend per customer.
- Subtract your total cost per order from your average spend per customer: this gives you your 12 month CLV.

(The next step towards a true CLV is to take the marketing spend out and allocate that back to each customer, e.g. if each email sent costs 20p, a customer should get "charged" 20p for each email they received.)

Hopefully you can see here the power of understanding your CLV. Here are a few common CLV findings to get you started:

- A customer who buys via two channels (shop and web) is worth double what a customer who buys via one channel is.
- A customer who doesn't shop seasonally (they shop with you all year round) is worth more than a customer who does.
- There will be one very expensive (per first order) recruitment tool (that you have probably stopped using) that only ever brought in profitable customers.
- Is frequency of order or value of order the most powerful for your profits?

Step 4: Third Core Foundation: Products and Promotions

Problems with your marketing plan are fairly easy to fix; if one thing isn't working it can be changed in a day or less, and there are always lots of alternatives to try. Problems with your products and promotions are much harder to fix, because it costs more and takes longer to fix such problems. Lead times for product supply are often long, and product is the place all your cash will get tied up. Many eCommerce businesses close every year due to cash flow problems because too much of their money has been tied up in stock that wasn't selling fast enough.

If you want your business to succeed, it's worth making sure you get your products and promotions right. That is exactly what we are going to cover in Step 4 of the eCommerce MasterPlan.

Why Are the Products So Important?

In Step 3, we talked about the margin and about making a profit. The margin you make and the profit you make is created by your products; created by the difference between how much you buy your products for and how much you sell them for, created by having the particular products your customers want to buy in stock, when they want to buy them.

For an eCommerce business, the products are the pieces of the business that actually physically exist: they are the substance of your business. You can get everything else right – customer service, marketing, fulfilment, price – but if the product isn't always right, year after year, you will lose the customer.

As we saw in Step 1, your Product Range Scope forms a critical part of your business strategy.

PRODUCT RANGE SCOPE

Niche ←――――――――――――→ Department Store

In many ways, the products you sell are your business, your brand. So it's really important to get them right. They are also the pulsing financial heart of your success; so not only do they need to be the right products, the numbers need to stack up, too.

Don't Ever Think You Can Tick Products Off the To-do List

Like marketing, your products need constant optimisation. You need to monitor the sales, and tweak the product mix, pricing, and promotion to keep the money rolling in and the warehouse emptying. Plus you will have suppliers changing their prices and service levels: no stock, too much stock, broken stock.

Optimisation is harder and more critical in products than in marketing, because more of what happens is outside of your control. A company I worked for had found the killer product for the summer season: an Indian-style parasol for the garden. It looked stunning, the photography was great, and the pricing and the margin were great, so it was decided to make it the main marketing image for the season. Out went the marketing, in came the orders. All was going really well. But then, a few were sent back, it turned out there was a fundamental problem, and the whole supply had to be recalled. All the existing orders were cancelled, all the customers who already had the product had to send it back, and we had to tell all further buyers (the catalogue was still landing!) that they couldn't have it. It was an unforeseeable nightmare that affected the whole business – from customer service and the warehouse right through to finance and marketing. However, it was a company with a very good Buying and Merchandising team, who knew that success wasn't based on one product, it was based on getting the mix right across the range, so the impact of the problem was considerably less than it could have been.

What Does This Product Mix Look Like?

WORKBOOK
Download our product mix plan workbook at **eCommerceMasterPlan.com/Free**

A product mix is a bit like customer segmentation; it includes lots of different facets, and getting it right means getting the right balance between each of the areas. In building and optimising the product mix, the following need to be in balance:

- Margin – first and foremost, this is ESSENTIAL to get right. If your target margin is 60%, then all your products should have a margin close to this.
- Number of suppliers – it saves so much time and effort if you deal with fewer suppliers.
- Product Categories – for example, a fashion retailer might know its units need to be split like this:
    20% skirts
    30% trousers
    40% tops
    10% coats
- Price points – for example your products need to fit within certain retail price points:
    30% under £10
    10% £10–20
    10% £20–40
    40% £40–75
    10% over £75
- Product range specific – e.g. sizing for fashion, colour for fashion, or anything that comes in multiple colours, memory size for MP3 players, or manufacturers for phone shops.

Most businesses will also keep 40–70% of the same products from season to season. So analysing the previous season's performance will guide you on how you need to optimise the mix for the next season: slightly fewer under £10, more blue ones…

The mix also needs to make your website and brand appealing to the customer, so you need to be following the trends and knowing what's coming up. In fashion, you need to know what the colours and styles of the coming season are; in hi-tech areas you need to know what is being released in the next season.

Your product mix helps define your brand, so it shouldn't change too radically year on year or you may lose your regular customers.

I Know What I Want to Stock, I Have Got the Product Mix Right: What next?

Next you need to work out how much of each item to buy. There is never unlimited money to buy stock, so the products you buy need to be the ones that are going to sell and meet the company objectives.

Forecasting and Cashflow

Any business selling physical goods needs to have an idea of how many of each item it will sell. Even if you are using Drop Ship suppliers (those that hold the stock for you and despatch direct to customers as you need them to) you need to give them an idea of how much of their stock you are going to sell.

It's really important to get the forecasting of sale (by item!) as accurate as possible:

- Your margin may be great, but if you don't have the products you can't sell them! So you need to make sure you have got stock.
- Backorders are expensive – they use up time and resources, and they annoy customers. So you need to make sure you have got the products in the warehouse before they are ordered by the customer.

You need the right amount of product, and you need it now, because until you have got it you can't sell it.

As the title of this section suggests, though, you also don't have unlimited cash and you'll almost always need to pay for the products before the customer pays you for them. Therefore you need to be really careful of what you buy this month, and what you buy next month.

Your marketing plan will help you work that out; if you are doing a big Valentine's Day promotion, then you need all your hearts, jewellery, chocolates, and champagne in the warehouse in January.

Two Clear Roles in Getting the Products Right

Put simply, to get your product mix right, you need to:

- Find products that your customer will like
- Make those products stack up into your product mix
- Buy the right number of units of each product
- Once they are on sale, respond to customer demand: not enough demand = discount; too much demand = buy more!

Generally, Part 1 will start up to about a year before the products actually go on sale, and Parts 2 and 3 are happening from about 6 months before the products are on sale until they are all sold out. The complexity of this means it's usually split into two roles. The Buying team look after Part 1, the Merchandising team look after Part 4 – and they collaborate to get Parts 2 and 3 right.

Product selection sits at the core of any eCommerce business because it influences everything else: finance, marketing, and the website itself.

Getting the Products Sold

Once the products are selected, they need to be promoted and put on the website. There are a few key things that can be done to increase the likelihood of customer purchase, and those are the quality of the pictures of the product and the nature of the information about the product.

The information about your products should be sufficient that all the customers' questions are answered, and that every barrier to purchase is removed.

For example:

- Dimensions – for furniture, the customer needs to know if it will fit in the room; for clothing the customer needs to know how long the jacket is, how long the trousers are, as well as normal sizing information.
- Add-ons – does it need batteries? If so, what batteries? How many? Are they included? This isn't just for batteries, it's for all sorts of products. If you buy a Dictaphone does it include a microphone? If buying a Filofax, does it include the contents? Does the holiday include the flights?
- Compatibility – will it work/fit with my existing items? What ports do the TV or laptop have?
- Maintenance – how often do I need to buy the printer cartridges, and how much would that cost? When do I need to get it serviced?

The questions that need to be answered will differ from product to product. A great way to find out what questions you need to address on the products page is to ask the people who talk to the customers – the call centre operatives, the shop staff – they can tell you what the customers are actually wanting to know. Online you can find out this information too – what are customers asking via social media? If you allow reviews of products, what are they saying?

As well as removing barriers to purchase, your product information should sell the product, so you need to write copy that will encourage the purchase.

The pictures can also do a lot to both encourage the sale and remove barriers to it. So make sure your pictures clearly illustrate the product; there are very few products for which just one image will do, as you almost always need the back and front view.

It is very worthwhile adding detail pictures: the buttons on a cardigan, a picture of the ports on the laptop, everything that comes in the box. The same is true for pictures of the product in action: have a picture of the trousers, and a picture of someone wearing them; a picture of the trowel and someone using it.

Photography is not cheap but it's worth investing in. Not only will good photography increase sales, it will also reduce returns of unwanted items because customers are less likely to buy the wrong thing.

The next step on is to have videos to illustrate the products. There are very few categories where video isn't going to help. Holiday websites benefit from films of the hotels and resorts, toy sellers benefit from showing the toys in action, and the fashion world benefits from mini-catwalk shows.

Some businesses even open this up to customer input. Firebox sell gadgets and modern homeware, and are fanatical about encouraging customers to provide videos and photos of themselves using the products – paying £50 for the really great ones. They also have fantastically detailed product information.

Promotions

> **WORKBOOK**
> get the Promotions workbook from the website
> **ecommerceMasterPlan.com/Free**

Whichever of the seven eCommerce Business Structures you are, and whatever your USP, you have to run some form of promotion. Promotions are not necessarily price discounts and, for some businesses, discounting would damage the brand, so we're talking about all those promotions that can be used to get customers to your site, and to buy. This might include:

- Free packing and postage
- Free returns
- Multibuys
- Voucher codes
- Sales
- 20% off deals
- Free gifts
- Half price when you do X
- Gift to charity
- Prize draw
- The last few available
- Brand new
- Previews

Before we dive into more details on these, there are a few rules to bear in mind when creating promotions to make sure a promotion works really well.

1 Margin

Any promotion shouldn't damage your margin. You don't want to do a Hoover[2] and give away something worth more than what the customer has paid. So only run a promotion if you know what it's going to cost you.

---

[2] The Hoover Free Flights Fiasco happened in 1992. Hoover launched a promotion in the UK giving two free airline tickets to anyone who bought £100 of Hoover products. This proved a very popular promotion, but had two problems: (i) many of the flights cost more than the customer had spent (ii) it was so popular Hoover ran out of some products. These two combined almost meant the end of Hoover as a business. You can read more about this on Wikipedia, where it has its own page!

2 Easy to understand
Keep it simple. A promotion should be easy for the customer to grasp or they won't take you up on it.

3 What do you want the customer to do?
Why you want to run the promotion and what you want the customer to do will change what promotion you put in place. If you need to clear out the rest of the season's stock to generate the cash to buy the new season's, then a sale with really simple discounting is a great idea. But if you want to increase the Average Order Value you need to do a multibuy offer or a "Spend over £X, Save £10".

4 End Date
Urgency is a great way to get people to do something, so promotions should mention an end date. Think "must end soon", "only 2 days left", "only available in June".

5 Which channels?
If you are Mail Order, Bricks and Clicks, or Full Multichannel: is the promotion going to run across all your channels or just online?

6 Which customers?
Do you want to run this offer for everyone, or just for your best customers? Or for those who you want to do something in particular? If you are working on upping AOVs, you could have a free gift which one group of customers gets if they spend £50, and another gets if they spend £100.

7 Spend Barriers
When you have to ship the product to customers it's always worth thinking about a spend barrier (must spend over Y to qualify). This will ensure you don't make a loss, and also mean the customers who respond are better customers, because they want more of your products.

If you think about each of these seven points before running any promotion, you'll get better results, it will cost you less, and will run more smoothly.

Key promotion types:

– Free Delivery
Really powerful: delivery is often a blocker to purchase, so offering it free is a great way to encourage the purchase.

– Sale
Generally you should only have a sale two to four times per year, when you need to clear out the old stock to make way for the new. It makes sense to tie in your sale times with the big boys in your marketplace because they set the customer expectation. A sale should also be available to all your customers, but you may want to give a single channel or group of customers an exclusive preview.

Never go to your maximum discount on day one – you want to leave room for further reductions.

– Category Offers

These are similar to sales, but are when you take only one product category and discount that: so, "20% off Swimwear" or "25% off Garden Furniture".

– Voucher Codes

To tightly control who can take advantage of an offer, and to track how well an offer is responded to, voucher codes can be really useful. So you could run the same offer for everyone, but give a different code to different customer segments.

Bear in mind that not everyone who responds to the offer will remember to use the voucher.

– Multibuys

A great way to encourage customers to get more involved with your brand, because it encourages them to spend more. It's also a good way to increase average order value. Be careful with these offers as it can be difficult to make them easy to understand online.

– Free Gifts

Free Gifts can be a great way to drive sales, but not all free gifts are created equal. A good free gift will be something that:

- fits with your brand
- has an RRP of between £5 and £10
- will appeal to your customers
- could be given as a gift by your customers
- light and easy to post (to keep your costs down)
- doesn't cost you very much – usually businesses will buy in products specifically as a free gift

And make sure you have got enough of the free product! There is little worse than having to spend lots of customer service time dealing with customers who you can't send their free gift to. Don't forget to put "while stocks last" in the Terms and Conditions.

Finally, don't forget to put the item on sale on the website – customers may well want to buy it.

– Half Price with Purchase

Similar to a multibuy and a free gift – but this encourages extra spend/the purchase of another item. So it's one or more products that can be bought at half price when the customer buys something else. Like a free gift it's worth sourcing these items specifically for the offer.

– Prize Draw Entries

This needs to be a compelling prize, but it can be a great way to motivate people to buy.

– Gift to Charity

When I worked at Barclays trying to get people to sign up to online banking, the best offer we ever ran was a £10 donation to Barnardos for each person who signed up in a month.

Charity donations can be a really great way to encourage customers to buy. Make sure you put a maximum donation in the Ts and Cs though.

– Last Chance to Buy
A lot of fashion shops are doing this now – a special category on the site where all the end of line stock is, still at the original price. This highlights an urgency to buy (a very powerful message) and also tidies up the rest of the website, putting the low stock items in one place.

– Preview/New
A new season launch/preview of a new range is a really compelling opportunity for your best customers.

There are many more ways to encourage customers to buy, and promotions don't have to be about savings. Do remember to keep a database of current promotions so you can avoid customers using several to get something for free!

Step 4 Complete: What Next?
Getting your products and promotions aligned gives any eCommerce business a great platform for profitable sales and growth. We've covered the three Core Foundations of any eCommerce business:

- Step 2 = Core Foundation 1, your website ✔
- Step 3 = Core Foundation 2, the big numbers ✔
- Step 4 = Core Foundation 3, products and promotions ✔

You should now know what you're selling, how much you need to sell, and on what website(s) it will be available.

That means it's time to get the marketing in place.

NOTES

What are the key points from this section?

Other Notes:

WEBSITE
Visit **eCommerceMasterPlan.com** for more information on product selection and promotional examples and ideas.

Step 5: I Have Built it – Why haven't they come? (aka Marketing!)

In the last three Steps, we built the three Core Foundations of every eCommerce business:

- The website
- The financial structure – Cost, Profit, and Growth
- The products and promotions mix

In Step 1 we identified what sort of eCommerce business you have.

Taking all this together enables us to understand what sort of marketing plan is going to work for you, and to build that plan.

When you rent a physical shop, part of your rent is actually marketing spend. You are buying your position in the place that people go shopping. Your shop's position guarantees you a certain amount of footfall (traffic), and your shop window brings you a certain exposure, allowing you to build some brand awareness.

When you mail a catalogue, or insert one in a newspaper or magazine, you are marketing to the list you have selected, but you are also building awareness of your brand in people other than those on your list. Catalogues get seen by multiple people, so you are attracting more than just those people already on your list.

Buying a URL (www.), building a website and hosting it somewhere brings you no traffic, no prospective customers. You still need to invest in marketing. For most eCommerce businesses, you will need to invest in offline marketing as well as online marketing if you want to grow fast and attract lots of customers.

What Sort of Marketing Are We Talking About?

There are nine key ways to market/get traffic to your eCommerce website. Not all nine ways are necessary for every business, and which ones you will need depend on your choices in Step 1.

– Content

By content, we mean video, blogs, articles, how-to guides, pictures, news, etc.

We have already touched on content as a way to differentiate your eCommerce business. It's also a great way to attract customers. Great content will improve your visibility on the search engines, and so bring you lots of traffic. It will also keep customers coming back to you when they need answers, so they will trust you and be more likely to buy from you than from the competition. Content is also key to getting customers to talk about you on social media; it's a great way to gain new customers, and increase your traffic from search engines. So content forms the basis of your own social media activity.

– Email

Email is of no use to you until you have someone to email.

Buying consumer email data is a massive waste of time and money because response rates are very, very low. So you need to use email marketing to keep your customers buying from you. Regular communications to keep customers up to date with your news and promotions are essential for a successful eCommerce business. But make sure to segment your data to be certain you are sending the right information to the right customers at the right time. It's also really important to be aware of the automatic emails that go out to customers (order confirmations, etc.) and make the most of those opportunities, too.

– Social Media

Social media can bring many benefits to an eCommerce business. It can:

- Attract new customers
- Build your relationship with existing customers
- Encourage repeat purchases
- Improve your traffic from search engines
- Help with customer service
- Build your brand

But you shouldn't do it unless you (i) have something to talk to your customers about (just promotional messages are not enough) and (ii) are ready and open for the two-way conversation that will come next. A Social media strategy is a big commitment, and it may take several months before it has an impact, so you need to be ready to commit to it for a long time before you see the reward.

– Brand Awareness

Unlike a shop or catalogue, a website by itself brings you no brand awareness at all.

So you have to invest in building awareness of your website. That might mean using other marketing methods such as advertising, direct mail, sponsorship or PR. But invest in it you must.

Brand Awareness provides a double-whammy benefit. It brings traffic to your website AND it means visitors to your website in general will be more likely to buy – because they know you, so they trust you a bit already.

Brand Awareness doesn't stop once the first purchase is made, though. You have to live up to your brand, so be aware of your brand impact post-purchase. The box the goods arrive in, the packing slip, the whole customer service experience.

– Offline

Most eCommerce businesses will need to do some offline marketing in order to recruit customers. Offline marketing frequently gives you a quicker, more cost-effective route to a much larger group of core customers than online marketing will. This includes:

- Trade shows
- Catalogue and Direct Mail
- Selling off the page in glossy magazines
- Other magazine advertising
- Advertorials
- PR

So don't forget to look away from the screen!

– Search

Many eCommerce businesses have been built on successfully capturing search traffic. There are some key foundations an eCommerce business needs to put in place to make the most of the search engine opportunity:

- Get the keywords on your website right. If you don't have the right keywords in the right places on your website, you are unlikely to appear in search results.
- Have content.
- If you have a physical location, create your "place page" – this a page on Google+ which adds you to location searches.
- Feed your product database into Google Base – this puts your products into the shopping results on Google.
- Enable people to talk about you online – Social Sharing is great for SEO.

– PPC – Pay Per Click

Pay Per Click is the fastest way to get quality traffic to your website. You can place ads on Google, Yahoo, and Bing that will appear to people searching for your products. You can place ads on Facebook that will appear to people interested in your products. It's really powerful. But it can also be very expensive.

You only pay when someone clicks on your advert, but you'll quickly be running hundreds of adverts. So you need to make sure which of your adverts are working, and which targeting methods (demographic and interests on Facebook, keywords on the search engines) are working, too. Optimising spend is a complex process: but done right it will bring you some great results.

– Remarketing

Of every 100 people who visit your website, fewer than 10 will leave you their details (by ordering or signing up to your social media or email). So 90 are leaving without a trace.

Remarketing is a way to encourage those 90 people back to your website. So if someone's been to your site and looked at dresses, you can place ads for your dresses in front of them on other websites. This is a highly effective way of gaining extra sales and making the most of all your other marketing activity – the activity that got them to your website in the first place.

Remarketing works in a very similar way to Google PPC, and can be run through the Google Adwords system.

– Partnerships

Partnering with other companies who target the same customer group as you can be hugely effective. There are many ways of doing this, and some are still very new.

The oldest method is Affiliate marketing: this is getting a suitable website to display ads for your eCommerce site, and paying them a commission on the sales made by customers they refer to you.

Increasingly there are now reciprocal agreements between companies. So you might swap an ad in your email with someone else. Ocado and Boden have such a scheme; when you have placed your order on Ocado, the order confirmation screen has an advert for Boden, and together with your groceries the delivery man drops off a co-branded mini Boden catalogue.

Partnerships don't have to be with other eCommerce sites, they might be with forums, newspapers and magazines, or even blogs.

How Do I Know Which Marketing Methods Are Important for My eCommerce MasterPlan?

With all the marketing methods that are available, it is necessary to focus on those that will work best for your business. To help you fast track to selecting the right ones for your business, we've created this handy table. Every method can be useful for every eCommerce operation, but here we've highlighted the ones you can't afford to ignore:

THE ESSENTIAL MARKETING METHODS FOR EACH ECOMMERCE BUSINESS STRUCTURE

	Content	Email	Social media	Brand	Offline	Search	PPC	Re-marketing	Partner-ships
Online Only	Y	Y	Y	Y		Y	Y	Y	
Mail Order		Y			Y	Y		Y	
Big Bricks and Clicks		Y		Y	Y	Y		Y	
Boutique Bricks and Clicks	Y	Y	Y		Y	Y		Y	
Piggy Back Niche									Y
Piggy Back	Y	Y	Y	Y					Y
Full Multi channel		Y		Y	Y	Y		Y	

So look at your current marketing activity, and ask yourself these questions:

- Which of the key areas for your eCommerce Business Structure are you already doing? How can you do them better?
- Which aren't you doing? Get started on them now!
- Finally, which marketing tactics are you using that aren't essential for your eCommerce Business Structure? How are they performing? Should you stop doing them or cut back in order to re-invest the money and effort in the right places?

The Marketing Must Fit with the Website

In Step 2, we talked about the following equation:

$$\text{Traffic} \times \text{Average Order Value} \times \text{Conversion Rate} = \text{Sales}$$

If the marketing isn't right, there will be no traffic, which means there is no business. Although much of the marketing can happen without affecting the website, the website has a job to do in attracting traffic as well as just converting it, so some of the marketing does involve changes to the website.

Creating your eCommerce Marketing MasterPlan

Before you get cracking with kicking off new marketing activity and stopping the old, you need to build a proper marketing plan. An eCommerce Marketing Plan should include both the channels you are going to use (e.g. email, PPC, or social media), plus the messages you will be using (e.g. sales, promotions, celerity tie-ins, Father's Day).

Before we run through HOW to build it, we should consider five things every good marketing plan is.

– A good marketing plan ... is very flexible.

Especially when we are dealing with online marketing activity: in 2011, Pinterest and Google+ barely existed, and now both have over 100 million active members and are driving quality traffic to retailers; in May 2012, Yahoo and Microsoft finally merged their PPC marketing platforms, opening up a viable alternative to Google Adwords for many more UK businesses. So you have to be ready to change your marketing plan to match shifting online conditions.

Before the plan can change, though, it actually needs to exist. It is so much easier to take advantage of new opportunities if you know what you need to change in order to do so. The best response to this ever-changing marketplace is to be even more rigorous in creating a marketing plan. Not bothering is not an option.

– A good marketing plan … will meet your objectives.

Some of these objectives we have already discussed (USPs, ROI, and number of orders). There are a number of others we will come to shortly. At the core of all eCommerce business objectives is driving sales and new customer acquisition.

Your marketing plan will take a range of activities into consideration to meet those objectives:

PLANS TO HIT YOUR OBJECTIVES

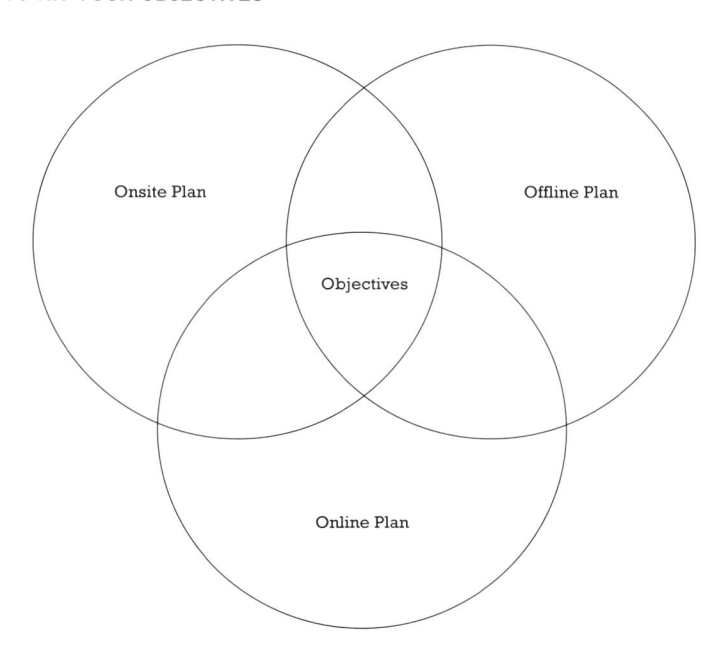

[Venn diagram with three overlapping circles labeled "Onsite Plan", "Offline Plan", and "Online Plan", with "Objectives" at the center intersection]

– A good marketing plan … recognises you have different types of customers.

From the very first sale, an eCommerce business has two types of customers: those who have bought and those who haven't – also known as your "Buyers" and your "Enquirers". These different groups of customers need to be marketed to in different ways, because the actions you want each of them to take are different:

| You need | Enquirers | to buy for the first time |
| You need | Buyers | to buy again |

This is a very simple form of **customer segmentation**, and, as your customer database grows, the segmentation will become more complex. Eventually, your customer segmentation will take into account when people buy, what they buy, how much they spend, where they live, their demographic profile, and much more. (See our tip box on eCommerce Customer Segmentation).

– A good marketing plan ... considers new and existing routes to market.

At the start of the section, we briefly outlined the nine core marketing areas for an eCommerce business and considered which are critical for each eCommerce Business Structure.

Some of these you may already be using, and if they are working you should keep them. Some that fit your eCommerce Business Structure you may not already be using, so the new marketing plan should include them, testing them first to make sure they work well enough for you. In online marketing, things are always cropping up and changing, so you just have to keep testing.

– A good marketing plan ... fits with your branding, your eCommerce Business Structure, and your USP.

It seems obvious but it's worth remembering: if your brand and USP is focused on customer service, trust, and honesty, keep the promotions simple and don't run "you could win a million" promotions. If you sell personal security products, don't buy cold email data.

Everything you do needs to fit your brand and USP.

Bear all these elements in mind as you run through the following Stages.

WORKBOOK
Please download the marketing plan workbook from the website to help you run through the following 5 stages – **eCommerceMasterPlan.com/Free**

There are 5 key stages to the marketing planning process:

- Researching where you and the market are right now
- Understanding your objectives
- Building the strategy and tactics into a plan of action
- Implementing the plan
- Reviewing the plan and amending it

Stage 1: Research

You need to understand where your business is right now, and also what's happening in the marketplace. Unless you understand these key areas, you won't know the foundations upon which you are building your eCommerce Marketing MasterPlan. And if you don't know what the foundations are, you are going to miss opportunities and risk building on soggy ground.

Key questions to answer in order to understand where your business is:

- **Your customers**
How many customers do you have? And how good are they?
How frequently do they buy? How much do they spend on an average visit? If you can get this figure, then understanding the Customer Lifetime Value (see the Tips Box in Step 3) can be particularly powerful.

- **Customer behaviour**
How many of your customers order online? And how are they different from your other customers?
Usually you will find in-store customers spend the least per visit, and catalogue customers the most. But online customers buy the most frequently. What do yours look like? It's particularly key to understand this if you want to migrate customers between channels: what are the opportunities and what are the risks, e.g. more sales value, but more orders to process?

- **Customer information**
What contact details do you have for your customers? And for how many of them? Do you have a working email address for everyone? For your best customers? Do you have postal addresses for your enquirers?

- **Marketing response**
How do your customers get to your website?
What's the trigger to them going there? Catalogues, in-store leaflets, search results, emails? Which traffic sources drive the most traffic to your website? Which traffic sources drive the best traffic? What promotions have you run in the past, and did they perform? Remember we want scale and ROI – so by best traffic, we mean that it drives lots of orders at a price we can afford.

- **Hard to measure marketing**
What other marketing are you currently doing and what impact is it having?
For some marketing activity, it's hard to measure the traffic, and it can take months/years before the traffic impact is felt. So you also need to be looking at how well these are already doing; this might include Facebook Likes, Twitter followers, column inches, mentions in magazines, or positions on search engines for your keywords.

MARKETING CHANNEL PERFORMANCE

	Site Visits	Sales	Orders	AOV	Costs	ROI
Email	10,000	1,000	50	20	500	100%
PPC	10,000	1,000	50	20	500	100%
Remarketing	10,000	1,000	50	20	500	100%
Search	10,000	1,000	50	20	500	100%
Search - Base	10,000	1,000	50	20	500	100%
Twitter	10,000	1,000	50	20	500	100%
Facebook	10,000	1,000	50	20	500	100%
Pinterest	10,000	1,000	50	20	500	100%

This table gives you an easy way to see how your marketing channels are impacting on your business's performance. You can do exactly the same for your promotions, too.

DOWNLOAD...
Grab a free Excel version from the website at
eCommerceMasterPlan.com/Free.

All the data for filling in this table should be at your fingertips – most of the figures are from your analytics and management accounts.

There are two key things you need to understand in your marketplace before you can identify your objectives:

1. What are your competitors doing?
What marketing have they been using? What products are they now selling? How have their prices and promotions been over the last year? Go and place some orders with them to see what their process is like. This can give you some ideas of things to test and also things to avoid!

2. What opportunities and threats are there in the marketplace?
What are you not doing that you should be? What do you need to be aware of: Royal Mail price increases, big national events, new routes to market, etc.?

Pulling all this information together will give you a great view of where you are right now, and what the next year may hold. I would really recommend putting it all in one place – be that in a document or in a folder (a real one, or an electronic one) so that when you need to review your plan you can easily see what your foundations were. Not only will that save you hours of time in the future, it will also make sure you don't miss anything the next time.

Stage 2: Objectives

In Step 3, we ran through how to set the Objectives for your eCommerce MasterPlan. Those are what we need to build the marketing plan to hit.

Stage 3: Strategy and Tactics, aka Creating the Plan

There are two ways to fill the gap in your marketing strategy:

- Do more of your existing activity: more emails, more keywords in Google Adwords, etc.
- Try out some new marketing areas

Section 2 will guide you through each of the marketing options and how you can make them work for your eCommerce business.

You should now have worked out what activity you will continue as per last year, what activity you will continue and invest more effort/money in, and what activity you will test or start. Now you can create the Plan.

Your Marketing Plan should be in three formats; this will make it easy to do the activity, monitor the activity, and make sure everyone involved knows what is happening. The easier you make it, the more likely it is to happen.

The three formats are:

A calendar of promotional activity
A month-by-month, or week-by-week series of activities in each marketing channel. That forms your checklist to make sure everything's happening. If you are struggling to get

started, put in what you did last year and the key dates for this year (Christmas, Easter, etc.).

A financial dashboard
A month-by-month performance tracker that has the cost and sales for each marketing channel AND your KPIs.

A written guide to the plan
It doesn't need to be more than a couple of pages but, if you have several people working on implementing the plan, it is critical to keep everything in line.

> DOWNLOAD...
> Examples of each of these are available on the website at
> eCommerceMasterPlan.com/Free.

AN EXAMPLE OF A SIMPLE PROMOTIONAL CALENDAR

	January				February			
	1-7	8-14	15-21	22-28	29-4	5-11	12-18	19-25
World Events			23rd Chinese New Year				14th Valentines	21st Shrove Tuesday
Last Year								
This year promotions								
Content								
Email								
PPC								

AN EXAMPLE OF A SIMPLE FINANCIAL DASHBOARD

Email	Sales	Budget	Costs	Budget	ROI	Budget
Jan	1,000	900	500	510	100%	76%
Feb	1,000	900	500	510	100%	76%
Mar	1,000	900	500	510	100%	76%
Apr	1,000	900	500	510	100%	76%
May	1,000	900	500	510	100%	76%
Jun	1,000	900	500	510	100%	76%
Jul	1,000	900	500	510	100%	76%
Aug	1,000	900	500	510	100%	76%
Sep	1,000	900	500	510	100%	76%
Oct	1,000	900	500	510	100%	76%
Nov	1,000	900	500	510	100%	76%
Dec	1,000	900	500	510	100%	76%
YTD	12,000	10,800	6,000	6,120	100%	76%

It is usual to work out a full 12-month marketing plan at once, but if that's too daunting, you are only in your first year of trading, or you just don't have the time, start with just a six-month or three-month plan. But DON'T FORGET to create the next three months or six months before you get to the end of the first one!

Stage 4: Implement

Now the marketing plan is in place you can get **implementing!**

So follow your plan, and kick off the first month's activity.

Stage 5: Review and amend

This is the most important step of the lot – you MUST measure how your eCommerce Marketing MasterPlan is going. The central secret to success in eCommerce is to keep optimising. And in order to do that you need to regularly review how each area of your marketing is working: including the website, the promotions, the channels, and the products themselves.

At the heart of this is the Financial Dashboard we created in Stage 3. That will tell you if performance is good or bad.

To understand why it's wrong or right you will need to delve deeper and look at the metrics we used to review performance in Stage 1. In Step 3 we ran through the details of analytics and how to use them effectively.

Top Tip: eCommerce Customer Segmentation

The first level of segmentation any eCommerce business should put in place is separating the Buyers and the Enquirers. It's a great first step to take because you will see an improvement in sales by treating these two segments differently. Plus, it's easy to tell who has and hasn't bought from you, so no matter how simple your systems are, it's almost always possible to segment your database this way.

We treat Buyers and Enquirers differently because we want them to do different things.

- The **Buyers** we want to buy AGAIN.
  They have already bought from us once, so we know a lot about them (name, address, email, what they bought, etc.), which means we can market to them much more effectively.
  They know us, they have taken the leap of faith and trusted us to provide them with the product/service they wanted and not to do bad things with their data. We have treated them well, and so built up a level of trust with them. So they are already predisposed to trust us (buy from us) again.

- The **Enquirers** we want to buy for the first time.
  They haven't ever bought from us, we don't know much about them, we might only have their email address. So we can't tailor the marketing to them very precisely; that means we're going to need to make a really compelling offer to get them to take the first leap of faith and buy from us.
  On the plus side, though, they do already know about us (they have visited the website and signed up for an email, or responded to an advert or similar). Not only do they already know about us, they want to know more about us – so they are ready to listen to what we've got to say.

Segmentation at the simplest level is straightforward to do, and its easy to see how to treat the different segments and what the likely benefits from that will be.

As you were reading through the Buyer and Enquirer descriptions, there were probably some questions floating around your head:

- What if they enquired a year ago?
- We ran that competition with X magazine last month and picked up lots of enquirers, but I think they might have been after the prize rather than us – what about these people?
- We have customers who only buy for Valentine's Day – what about them?
- Some of our customers buy in store, phone to order, and use the website – what about them?
- Men buy gifts from us at Christmas, but not during the rest of the year.
- We have customers who buy low-priced items from us every month, but others who spend LOTS in one order every six months – should we treat them differently?

All of these are great questions to be asking – and show just how much you can do with your segmentation. They highlight the most difficult thing about segmentation, too: if you try to implement everything now you'll drive yourself (or your marketing team) insane. It's too much do all in one go, and, because there is so much going on, you will find it really hard to work out what is actually working and what isn't.

Build your Segmentation Plan

WORKBOOK
Download our Segmentation Plan workbook at
eCommerceMasterPlan.com/Free

You need to plan the implementation: in what order are you going to tackle the stages of segmentation? Our outline of the key segmentation options provides you with a checklist of segmentations to use with your data. Start at the top and just work your way through them. Not all will be relevant for your business, so look at the data to work out which you should use and pay attention to.

We have started with the four segmentations that mail order businesses have been using for decades to build their businesses effectively: RFM, which stands for Recency, Frequency, Monetary Value.

- Buyers vs. Enquirers – a no brainer, very effective, and very easy to do.
- Recency – how recently did they buy/enquire? The more recently someone last interacted with the business, the more likely they are to buy again. Suggest doing this in 6-month to 12-month blocks.
- Frequency – how frequently do they buy? Once a year, three times a year, ten times a year? You will need to investigate your database to find the right segmentation for this group. As well as trying to get the next purchase, you are aiming to increase their frequency.
- Monetary Value – how much do they spend each time they buy? Under £25? £26 to £50? Over £50? Again, you will need to investigate your data to find the right splits for you. Of course, you are also trying to get these customers to spend more with you; if they normally only spend £25 you want them to start spending over £25.

Buyers/Enquirers plus RFM forms a very solid foundation for your segmentation. You should map your customers in these segmentations in a matrix like the one below in order to see where the clumps of data are.

DOWNLOAD…
you can download an excel version of this from
eCommerceMasterPlan.com/Free

EXAMPLE RFM SEGMENTATION

Only purchased once

Last Order > AOV	0-6m	7-12m	13-18m	19-24m	25-36m	37-42m	42+
£0-30							
£30-60							
£60-100							
£100+							

Purchased twice

Last Order > AOV	0-6m	7-12m	13-18m	19-24m	25-36m	37-42m	42+
£0-30							
£30-60							
£60-100							
£100+							

Purchased three times

Last Order > AOV	0-6m	7-12m	13-18m	19-24m	25-36m	37-42m	42+
£0-30							
£30-60							
£60-100							
£100+							

Purchased more than three times

Last Order > AOV	0-6m	7-12m	13-18m	19-24m	25-36m	37-42m	42+
£0-30							
£30-60							
£60-100							
£100+							

The other segmentation options look more deeply at buyer behaviour:

- Source of the data – this is really useful with Enquirer data because it will show you which of your enquiry generation methods capture the best data (so was that magazine competition worth it? Or was the small advert in the *Sunday Times* better?). It's also really good to continue to track this once they become buyers, because then you know where your best buyers come from.
- Seasonality – when they buy: do they only buy at Christmas, or only in the summer? In which case, you either only market to them when they buy OR you need to try to convert them to buyers outside the key season.
- Products – what of your range do they buy? Jewellery or Furniture? The vacuum cleaner or just the bags for it?
- Purchase type – are they buying for themselves or as a gift?
- Multichannel – does the customer use all your channels to buy, or just one?
- Marketing response – you can't track this in every channel, but with email you can track who is opening and who is clicking your emails.
- Customer Service Usage – are they a "good" or a "bad" customer? This could also be returns rate or cancelled orders information.
- GeoDemographics – male or female, age, where in the country, MOSAIC profiling, or similar.

With all this segmentation you should always be asking:

- Which segments make up the best customers, and how do you keep them?
- Which segments make up the worst customers – and is it worth marketing to them at all? (Is someone who only ever spends £10 and orders only once a year worth the marketing expense?)
- Is our segmentation structure right? Should we go into more detail, or less?

Step 5 Complete: What next?

Congratulations! You have now completed the 5 Steps to building your eCommerce MasterPlan.

This is only the start of your eCommerce journey. The power of your MasterPlan lies in you constantly optimising what you are doing: optimising the website, the products, the finances, the marketing.

Don't forget to ask yourself, whenever there is an important decision to be made:

- "Does this fit with my eCommerce Business Structure?"
- "Does this change my Product Range Scope?"
- "Does this help build my USP?"

NOTES

What are the key points from this section?

My eCommerce Business Structure critical marketing activities are:

My USP marketing activities are:

Other Notes:

Next Steps

First, read through the following marketing methods that fit with your eCommerce Business Structure and USP to learn more about the marketing activity you need to be doing.

Second:

> **WEBSITE**
> Visit **eCommerceMasterPlan.com** for more information and case studies of businesses with different eCommerce Business Structures, Product Range Scopes, and USPs.

> **WEBSITE**
> Don't forget to sign up for the emails from eCommerceMasterPlan.com to make sure you get the latest news of what's happening in eCommerce straight into your inbox.

Section 2:
Key Online Marketing Methods

Content Marketing

Content marketing is essential for these eCommerce Business Structures:

- Online Only
- Boutique Bricks and Clicks
- Niche PiggyBack

It is also particularly useful if your USP is:

- Knowledge and Information – because it's central to building a reputation for knowledge and information.
- Customer Service – part of customer service is providing customers with the information they need.

Why Should You Use Content Marketing if you are an eCommerce Business?

Content marketing is a form of marketing that will have a positive impact on many areas of the business, and once you have built your great content it's very hard for a competitor to beat you on that front, so it becomes a great way to maintain and grow your share of the market. However, it does take a lot of time and effort to build a good content base, and you must keep it up to date, too. Content marketing is powerful on a number of levels:

- It provides you with a USP that is very hard to copy.
- Providing great content will mark your website out as a fantastic source of useful information, not just another eCommerce website. So it can really enhance your brand and customers' perception of you.
- Great content is an essential foundation of a social media strategy – social media is all about sharing and conversions. So you need something to talk about and something to share – that's the job of the content.
- It's a way to use the great knowledge that already exists in your business.
- Content is also essential to a successful Search strategy. It will act as "link-bait", encouraging other people to link to your website. It will also provide pages and pages that will attract the search engines, and contain lots of keywords.
- Having content will enable your other marketing strategies to be more interesting and drive better results; you'll have something other than products to talk about in emails and offline marketing, you'll have more traffic to re-market to, too.
- Finally it will bring you a steady stream of traffic that's interested in your products and business, month in, month out.

Content Marketing Objectives for eCommerce Businesses

The impact of your content marketing will be hard to measure – but that's no excuse for not having objectives. The key to successful content marketing is to keep producing new content. It may take a long time (6–12 months) before you see real sales gains.

Your key objectives will be to attract traffic to your website through the content, and to create sales activity from that traffic. You should also have clear targets for content creation.

As we have seen above, though, content will impact on lots of other areas of your marketing; so it is hard to isolate and track exactly what impact the content itself will be having. Some of its impact will be felt through Search, through social media, and other marketing channels.

The key objectives will be how much the content is read (the page views) and the overall turnover improvements.

How Content Marketing Works

At its most simple, content marketing is creating content that relates to your brand/products and putting it on your website. That might be a guide to buying the perfect jeans, or how to install a dishwasher, or it might be an opinion on an article on the solar technology of the future.

That content could be a PDF, a blog post, an infographic or a video. It might not only be on your website – it might be on your blog, YouTube, Slideshare, or someone else's blog.

Every piece of content you create should do at least one of these things:

- Be something people will read and want to share – either by Tweeting, or linking to it
- Reflect your brand well, enhancing it by supporting what you stand for and positioning you as an expert in your field
- Help sell the products – removing barriers to conversion, like a sizing guide, or a catwalk video
- Appeal to your target customers

One very simple tactic I have seen is by the company BrightMinds, who sell educational toys and games. On their website you can download SAT past papers for free. That's awesome content for a business that is targeting parents interested in helping their children learn.

What is Content?

Before creating your Content Marketing Plan, here are some ideas of what content can be:

- Infographics – these are pictorial displays of data, and are very popular. There are lots getting shared already on social media platforms.
- Guest Blogging – this can be a great way to get content, or spread your content. You may want to find someone to guest blog on your website, or go guest-blogging yourself. This is a great way to increase customers' perception of your expertise.
- YouTube – the second largest search engine in the world. And it's owned by Google. So if you are creating videos, why not upload them here? You can easily then embed them in your own site too, so it saves on hosting costs as well.
- Photos – there are lots of great photo hosting sites, like Flickr. With Instagram and Pinterest around now, it's also important to make sure your images are easily shared.
- Slideshare and Scribd – these are two sites where you can upload documents to be shared. So how-to guides, and presentations are well worth putting up here.

WORKBOOK
There is a workbook for creating your content marketing plan available on the website at **eCommerceMasterPlan.com/free**

How to Create your Content Marketing Plan

Content marketing is much simpler than people assume. Most businesses have more content than they think, so this plan helps you identify it and plan it – and that's the hard bit! It is much more difficult than creating it.

What content can you/should you create?

Before you can do anything else with your content marketing, you need to work out what content you are going to produce. To do this you need to do a brainstorm with everyone in the business to see what content you already have, and what should be produced. Ask everyone:

- What content do we already have?
- What content would our customers appreciate having on the website?
- What stories are there around our products?

Take the answers and extrapolate them. The chances are that from the brainstorm there won't be a vast number of stories; that's because people are simplifying it. Each story that's on the brainstorm can create several items of content. For example:

HOW ONE IDEA BECOMES LOTS OF CONTENT

Initial ideas	
Photo Shoot for Summer Season	New Google Nexus Tablet released
Content Items	
• Photos of the shoot • Video from the shoot • Competition to decide the location of the shoot • Competition for a customer to be a model • Competition for a customer to style one of the shots • Competition for a customer to win all the clothes used in the shoot • Guess the location • We're off to the shoot tomorrow, really excited about the new range • Outtakes from the shoot • The models' perspectives on the product	• Tablet available on 15th July 2012 • Why you shouldn't buy the Google Nexus • Why you should buy the Google Nexus • Comparing the Google Nexus with the other two top tablets of the moment • First impressions of the Google Nexus • Unboxing the Google Nexus • Pictures of what's in the box • Product pictures from all angles • Three odd uses for the Google Nexus • Will the Nexus survive being dropped off the roof? • Top five great things about the Google Nexus • Three things Google will need to do better with their next tablet

Each idea you have has the potential to be turned into several different pieces of content in varying formats.

Decide your content formats/what platforms you are going to use

Now you have an idea of the sort of content you are going to be creating, you need to decide what formats, and what platforms, you are going to be using.

For most businesses, the starting point, the centre of your content strategy, is your blog. A blog can host pictures, text, audio, and video, which makes it really versatile.

Ideally it should be located at www.yourdomain.com/blog; then the search engines see it as part of your website. If you can't do that for hosting reasons, then use blog.yourdomain.com: this will be classed as a separate website by the search engines, so you need to make sure you have plenty of links back to the eCommerce website.

Blog content is then very easy to syndicate, feeding into your social media activity (see page 109).

If you are also going to be creating video, audio, images, presentations, etc., then to get the most from that you want to be putting it on websites as well as your own:

- Video => YouTube
- Photos => Flickr
- Audio => YourListen.com
- Presentations => Slideshare or Scribd

This will mean your content starts pushing people to your website, not just pulling them in. So you get double the benefits.

Now you should have a long list of story ideas, and a list of where you are going to be putting that content. So now we need to turn that into a calendar of activity, to make sure it gets done!

Create your Content Marketing Calendar

This is really simple: map out what story you are going to be putting live for each week of the year, and where it's going.

DOWNLOAD...
There's an example you can download from the website at
eCommerceMasterPlan.com/Free

AN EXAMPLE OF A CONTENT MARKETING CALENDAR

	January				February			
	1-7	8-14	15-21	22-28	29-4	5-11	12-18	19-25
World Events				23rd Chinese New Year			14th Valentines	21st Shrove Tuesday
Last Year								
This Year Stories								
Blog Post								
Video								
Audio								
Docs/ Presentations								

Get going!

Now you have built your content marketing plan, you just need to implement it. So make sure everyone who needs to be creating the content is ready and understands their deadlines.

Don't think that you need to be able to do all of this in-house. There are great copy-writing services out there that will quickly learn your tone of voice and pull together your blog posts and other content for you. It's well worth investigating this.

When Doesn't Content Marketing Work?

Content marketing will have a positive affect for any business; but that doesn't mean it's always worth doing it. You have to invest a lot of time (and often money, too) into getting your content created and distributed. So will it bring you enough benefit (sales) to be worth it?

There's no easy way to answer that question, but there are some circumstances in which it's less likely to be as effective for you:

- Regulated marketplaces – if you are selling regulated products, like pharmaceuticals or insurance, there are many restrictions on what you can say about your products. That means it's going to be harder to come up with ideas, but also that the creation process will be more expensive because you have to get everything checked by compliance.
- Cheap Commodity products – like toothpaste, bottled water, pencils. These are products that people just want to buy; they are cheap enough that it's not worth shopping around, and they don't need extra information on them. People aren't going to be interested in consuming the content, so it won't be so useful. To succeed with content here, you either need a very exciting idea or you need to spend a lot on building the momentum.

What to Measure in Content Marketing

CONTENT MARKETING PERFORMANCE REPORT

Entry Point	Visits	Bounce Rate	Orders	Value	AOV	Conversion Rate	Sales / Visit
blog	5,000	30.00%	26	1,820	70	5.00%	36.4p
video	5,000	35.00%	35	1,575	45	8.00%	31.5p

As we discussed in the Objectives section at the start of this Step, it's very hard to separate out the impact of your content separately from your social media, or search, or other marketing activity. So we have to be a bit clever in the way we measure it. The table above is a simple way to measure the effectiveness of individual pieces of content; by tracking results in analytics at the point where people entered the website, rather than how they got there. The big picture for the content, though, is how well the whole marketing plan functions.

Below are the key metrics you need to be measuring for your Partnership marketing; most are in the table above:

CONTENT MARKETING METRICS

Metric	What is it?	Benchmarks
Visits	The number of visitors getting to your website as a result of each piece of content. That might be visitors from YouTube or SlideShare, or somewhere else that's hosting your content. Or it might be people entering the site via the blog.	There is no benchmark as such for this, but it should be increasing month to month, and driving an increasing percentage of total site visits.
Bounce Rate	A percentage A bounce is someone who gets to your website, looks at one page, and then leaves – it's a good indicator of what quality your content is, and how well it's encouraging people further into the website	A good Bounce Rate is below what your website achieves overall
Orders	The number of orders placed as a result of the activity Tracked via Google Analytics	
Conversion Rate	A percentage Orders divided by Clicks	This should be in line with your website's average Conversion Rate
Sales	The value of the orders	
AOV	The average order value Sales divided by Orders	Partly depends on what you are promoting in the email. But generally should be online with normal AOVs.
Sales per Visitor	A great way to compare the performance of activity where the traffic volume varies Sales divided by Visitors	
Email sign-up	The number of these visitors who sign up to hear more from you	Content marketing isn't entirely about driving the first sale, it's more about increasing your potential customer base; so it's important to also track how many extra email sign-ups you get as a result of the activity

Successful Content Marketing Checklist:

- What content do you have already?
- What content could you produce/should you produce?
- Choose the right mediums – video, text, image.
- Create a content creation calendar – and stick to it!
- Track what content works best, and do more of that.
- Get customers to create your content, too.

NOTES

What are the key points from this section?

Other Notes:

WEBSITE
Visit **eCommerceMasterPlan.com** for the latest information on Content Marketing, and more guides to how Content Marketing could work for you.

Email Marketing

Email marketing is essential for these eCommerce Business Structures:

- Online Only
- Mail Order
- Big Bricks and Clicks
- Boutique Bricks and Clicks
- Niche PiggyBack
- Full Multichannel

It is also particularly useful if your USP is:

- Knowledge and Information – because it's a great way to show how much you know.
- Customer Base – email is a powerful way to keep your customer base active, and the larger your customer base, the more effective email can become through segmentation.

Why Should You Use Email if you are an eCommerce Business?

Email marketing is one of the most effective ways to make money in eCommerce Marketing. It's powerful on a number of levels:

- You get the results almost instantly – people will buy within minutes of the email launching.
- You are in total control – you are in control of the products, promotions, and stories you are putting in front of people, you are in control of when it goes out, and of which customers get the message. All this means you have a lot of influence over what the outcomes are; which products get bought, how much you sell, and more.
- You can target specific customer groups, so getting lapsed customers to buy again, or those who've enquired to buy.
- It should always be profitable – there are so many levels of technology that you should always be able to find a solution that means you are making money.

Email Marketing Objectives for eCommerce Businesses

Email activity should be focused on hitting your big objectives, right from the first email you send. It needs to be driving the sales for you, and it needs to be keeping your customers active, getting them to buy again and again.

As you grow the list size and complexity of your email activity you can then focus campaigns on increasing AOV, improving customer segments, and more. It's a very flexible tool, but remember: its Number One job is to drive the sales.

How Email marketing works

What you control	Why is it important?
Software and Hosting	Gets your email into the customers inbox
From name	Builds trust and recognition
Subject Line	Gets the email opened
Content & structure	Gets the customer to the website
Story/Message	Defines how powerful the email will be
Segmentation	

The aim of every email you launch is to get the customer to the website, as quickly as possible. If they don't click to the website, they can't buy. The faster they get to the website, the more likely they are to buy.

You need to get first four listed on the left correct for every email you send; they are the bedrock to your email performance and, if they are not right, your email marketing will not drive the volume of sales it should. The real power, though, is in the Story and the Segmentation.

The **Story** is what the whole email (or series of emails) is about: it might be Sale, it might be Spring collection, it might be Time to Stock up the Bird Table. Getting a strong story at the right time will really increase sales.

The **Segmentation** is which customers you send the email to.

The best ever return I achieved from an email was when we identified customers who had previously bought similar items, and sent them an email specifically about a new range of those items. The email only went to about 1,500 customers but the ROI was off the scale. This was a niche product, so segmenting the 1,500 customers off to receive their own message meant we could send the rest of the database (80,000) a more general message, thus getting a better response from them than we'd have got if we'd sent the niche message to everyone.

Of course, we also had the Software, Hosting, From Name, Subject Line, and Content and Structure correct – which all helped, but it was getting the Story and Segmentation right that made the performance so strong.

Who to Email

Before we get into each of the above in more detail, I just want to make it really clear that everything in this section is about emailing YOUR list. That means emailing the people who have bought from you (the Buyers), and those who have subscribed to your emails, but not bought yet (the Enquirers).

Cold emailing is not worth the effort. This is because:

1. Response rates are low and prices are high, so you are unlikely to recruit new customers cost effectively.
2. Data quality is poor – if you go for the cheap lists you are going to get bad data, and mailing to that is a waste of your time.
3. You could mess up your emailing to your own list – this is explained more on page 91, but your likelihood of getting into the inbox is based on how well received your emails are; so if you mail some cold data and three people on Hotmail hit the "Spam" button, you might not get any emails to people using Hotmail for months. That could prove to be very expensive.

You need to grow your own database, encouraging sign-ups to your newsletter and making sure you have got the right email data from your customers.

If you do decide you want to do some cold emailing, the most important thing is not to use the same software that you use to send your normal emails; that way the performance of your house file is protected. You should have a separate email service provider for this, or get the data from someone who will manage the launch for you. There are a handful of routes that may be worth testing:

– Appending

This is quite a clever method, where you use an appending service to find the email addresses of customers you don't have an email address for. If your customer database has lots of missing or email addresses, or ones not working, this might be worth considering.

The process is usually that the Appending Company will take your customer database and match it with theirs, then contact those customers to see if they are happy to sign up for your emails. The good thing is that once you have got the data to use it is opted in, and you have a potential customer – so the response should be good. But, it isn't a cheap service; the price reflects the complexity.

– Surveys

There are many companies who will run a survey on your behalf to help you collect data. Those filling in the survey will be asked questions agreed to by you, and have the opportunity to sign up to your emails. You then get the email addresses of those who wanted to sign up.

You can gather a volume of emails quite quickly, but the quality is not always great. Those filling in the surveys are often habitual survey respondents; they are signing up to lots of companies, so it's less likely you will get a strong response from them. The questions in the survey help you work out which data you actually want to buy; so, if you sell women's clothes, you don't want to buy the men's data. That is fine, but the company running the survey only get paid for the data you take, so expect them to want to keep the survey pretty generic so you receive lots of data.

– Partnering/Buying Space in Someone Else's Email

We will be writing more about this in Section 2, but basically it means paying another company to promote you in their emails. In some cases, you will be able to swap a promotion rather than pay for one. As with all partnering, make sure you are both after similar customer types.

If you do any of these data capture methods, make sure you keep the data collected in a separate list so you can monitor how it really performs.

Making Your Email Marketing Successful

WORKBOOK
Download the Email Marketing Workbook from the website at
eCommerceMasterPlan.com/Free

Software and Hosting

It's critical to choose the right method of launching your emails. Which Email Service Provider (ESP) you choose will have a major impact on the performance of your email marketing. This is because the quality of your ESP determines whether or not you make it to your customer's inbox or get put into their junk box, or not delivered at all. ESPs also come in very different price brackets, so you need to choose the one that fits your needs and budget now. The good thing is that as your email becoming more complex and your need for more functionality is driven by the size of the list, this also drives your sales volume; so your sales should grow as your costs grow, meaning it's always profitable.

> **DOWNLOAD...**
> On the website there is a brief guide to ESPs and which suit what size of business. You can find that at **ecommerceMasterPlan.com/Free**.

Getting into the inbox is based on how companies like Hotmail and Gmail view the black box (IP address) and from address (@email.yourbrand.com) that your email comes from. Their point of view is primarily based on how they have previously seen you perform. How many times their customers have marked your email as spam; how well their customers respond to your emails. There is a lot you can do to make sure your performance is good:

- Suppress hard bounce notifications
- Suppress 'report as spam' requests from ISPs
- Suppress inactive data – the 'emotionally dormant'
- Monitor performance of all data segments
- Use multi-part messages (using HTML and text preference fields)
- Have optimal text to image balance
- Use email layouts that appeal to consumers
- Have email content/ messages relevant to the consumer
- Double check emails against spam tools pre-send
- Have an obvious 'unsubscribe' link(s) on the email
- Use a consistent 'From Name'

A great deal of this is down to managing your data well (hence the advice against doing any cold mailings through your normal ESP). Having a better ESP will also help; the better your ESP's whole relationship with the likes of Hotmail, the better chance your emails will have of getting into the inbox.

We will discuss data in more detail when we come onto segmentation, but there are two things you should do with your data to keep it clean, and keep your SenderScore up:

- Remove emails that don't work, or of customers who don't like you any more – the faster your unsubscribe system works the better
- Don't keep mailing to data that are not responding. If someone hasn't opened any of your emails in over six months, stop sending to them. They have effectively unsubscribed. We call these "emotionally dormant"; these are the people most likely to mark you as spam, and Hotmail etc. often hold on to dead accounts as "spam traps" – and you don't want to be mailing into a spam trap. (Of course, do occasionally send really strong messages to this group as you could get a few converting.)
- Across the lists I have done this on, it has reduced send volumes by over 50%, and has made no impact on sales; it's going to save you money and increase ROI, too.

Email deliverability is vital to the success of your campaign. Your potential customers need to be able to see your email in order to make a purchase. Maintaining this deliverability is down to two things: the ESP (the software and hosting) you choose, and how you use your data.

If you want to see how you are currently doing then check your SenderScore (see the Tips Box on page 106).

When you are selecting your ESP, you need to ask these questions:

- What is the cost structure?
  Monthly fee, set up costs, price per 1,000, etc.: price structures vary a lot, so make sure you know exactly what you are going to be paying for.
- What's their data policy?
  What data will they/won't they allow you to upload? For some, you sign to agree to the provider's policies, and others actually put technical blocks in place – so you can't upload info@ email addresses or similar. All of this is good news, and is worth knowing about.
- Can they integrate with your systems?
  Do you need this? If so what are the costs?
- What is their average SenderScore?
  You need to know how good they are at getting your emails to the inbox of your customers.
- Segmentation flexibility
  How can you manipulate your data in their system? The very cheapest may only allow you one list; so no segmentation. The most complex allow you to auto-segment and build very complex mailing plans.
- What will your sending email address be?
  @yourbrand.com or @email.yourbrand.com. Or @theirbrand.com?
- Analytics tracking
  Does their system automatically tag all the links in your email so you can see the traffic easily in your analytics system (e.g. Google Analytics)?
- The help service
  How can you get help: by phone, email, or forum?
- How long are you tied in for?
  As your list grows and your business develops, you might want to change ESP. Can you?
- How complex is it to leave?
  Can you literally just export your html and database? Or is it harder than that?

If you want to go all-out on maximising your deliverability, there are two further things you can do: set up the SPF records on your domain and get into White Lists.

A White List guarantees you are put into the inbox of your customers. The best White List is Return Path's SenderScore Certified. It's not cheap, but if you have a large list it may well be worth it. The criteria for entry are a series of standards you need to meet and adhere to, and they are set pretty high, so becoming compliant may take some time, too.

SPF is the Sender Policy Framework. It's a way to define where your legitimate emails are sent from. Not all email recipients check this, so it's not critical, but it's worth doing it if you can.

From Names

Thankfully From Names are much more straightforward than Software and Hosting.

Your From Name is important because it is one of two things that are going to make the customer open your email: the subject line will be the reason someone opens, but if the From Name is wrong, the customer won't get as far as the subject line.

The job of the From Name is to be recognised and trusted; it's the constant part of your email marketing. So once you have chosen your From Name you should stick with it. The From Name you should go with should usually be your company name, because that is the most recognisable From Name you have got. For some businesses, though, it might be the founder's name: for example, if you got an email about a follow-up to this book, would it perform better if the From Name was "Chloë Thomas" or "eCommerce MasterPlan"? I don't yet know the answer to that – but I will be testing it.

If your product range is quite vast (you are at the department-store end of the scope) or you email on very different topics, you might want to have a subject line that changes a bit. So if you sell men's and women's clothes, you might want to use "brand name women" and "brand name men" as your From Names. Etsy have a range of emails customers can sign up to, and each has a different From Name:

> Etsy Success – is advice on how to sell more
> Etsy Dudes – is Etsy products for men
> Etsy Finds – is the daily cool products found to Etsy email
> Etsy Labs – learn from other people on Etsy

....

Subject Line

The Subject Line has one job: to get your email opened. By the right people.

So it either needs to be intriguing or obvious:

> Intriguing = "It's All Gone Tribal"
> Obvious = "Sale Now On – Save up to 70%"

Your Subject Line also needs to attract the right people: those who are going to be interested in the content and buy.

You can find countless blogs and white papers on what does and doesn't work in Subject Lines. These are useful for one reason and one reason only: to give you some ideas of what you might want to test. There isn't a perfect subject line out there; there is only the best Subject Line you can use at a given time to advertise a given set of products.

But you can start to work out some rules for your business. Key things to test are:

- Case – Title Case (where the initial letters are all capitals), or Sentence case (where just the first letter is a capital), or all lower case.
- Include your brand name? It is probably already in the From Name.
- Length – long or short? Every subject line should be visible all at once, so you do need to keep it relatively short.

- How obscure can you go?
- Personalisation – does performance improve when you include the person's name in the Subject Line?

If your list is big enough, you can test for every email you send; separate out some of the data (at least 10k), split it in half, and send each half a different subject line. Twenty-four hours later, send the rest of the data the one that worked best.

If you are going to test subject lines, select your winner based on the performance of the whole email, not just the open rate. We want the right people opening, not just anyone. So look at the following statistics:

- Open rate
- Click rate
- Conversion rate
- AOV
- Sales per delivered

The last one is the most important: if you take the sales from the email segment and divide it by the number of people the email went to, you get a great way to compare the segments. Here is an example.

EMAIL SEGMENTS PERFORMANCE

Subject Line	Delivered	Opened	%	Clicked	%	Orders	Value	AOV	Conversion Rate	Sales / Delivered
A	5,000	1,500	30.00%	525	35.00%	26	1,820	70	5.00%	36.4p
B	5,000	1,750	35.00%	438	25.00%	35	1,575	45	8.00%	31.5p

Even though Subject Line B had a higher open rate, Subject Line A drove a better return, with a Sales Per Delivered of 36.4p vs. 31.5p. So the right Subject Line to roll out would be A, because it drove the right people to open, and those people bought.

Content: The body of the email

Once people have opened the email, you want to get them to the website as quickly as possible; within seconds, ideally.

So the structure of your email needs to be designed to encourage customers to click. It needs to make it easy for them to click, and to show your products off in a way that encourages the click.

There are some things that work well in pretty much every eCommerce business's emails. Make sure you have some compelling text links at the top of the email: this might be your category headings, or it might be some Preview Pane text – that's a line of text repeating the subject line (or is similar to it) that links directly to the page on the website about the subject. Preview Pane text should be to the top left of the email so that it appears in the preview pane whether the customer has their system set up to put that below or to the right of the rest of their emails.

Email Marketing | 99

Most customers will click on the content either towards the top or the bottom, so put your best products there and don't spend too long building up the middle. Very long emails are generally not a good idea (but do test them). Do include prices of the products you feature, and if they are on sale or offer show the before price too. Make anything that can be linkable a link: prices, product name, images, all of it.

Text is good in emails because not everyone downloads the images. If you can get them to click before they have downloaded the images that's a good thing. Having a good balance between text and image can also help get your emails delivered, but if you are on a very good ESP and have a strong SenderScore that is less important.

For every marketing email you send, create a text version and an HTML version; it should be obvious how to do this within your ESP's software, so make sure you do it. It improves deliverability and response. Often once you have got the HTML built you can automatically create the text version – so it's not that hard to do either!

There are a few things that are good/legally essential to include in every email you send; this is the content you put "above" and "below" the email:

Put at the Top	Put at the Bottom
Preview Pane Text (see above)	Unsubscribe
Add us to your safe senders list	What email address the email was sent to
If you can't see the images click here (with a link to an online version of the email)	If you are a UK limited company, your registered name, address, company number, and the region you are registered under
Link to a mobile version (the text version)	Terms and Conditions for any promotion or competition if required
	Customer service contact details
	Links to your social media profiles

> **DOWNLOAD...**
> We have copy and paste examples on the website at
> **eCommerceMasterPlan.com/Free**

Once you believe you have got a good email design, you need to check how it renders. You have just built some HTML coding that pulls words and images and links together in a certain way, but that HTML is open to interpretation. The different email systems will interpret it in different ways, so you need to know how well it is being interpreted before you send it to your customers.

To do this, set up an account with each of the systems your customers use to receive your emails. For example:
- Cloud-based email might include:
  - Hotmail
  - Google Mail
  - Yahoo mail
  - AOL (hard to get an account with)

- Desktop-based email may include:
  - Outlook 2003 and 2007
  - Thunderbird
- Mobile-based email may include:
  - Blackberry
  - iPhone
  - iPad
  - Android systems
  - Microsoft systems, including Surface

Next, send a test version of your email to each of the accounts you have set up, and go and see how it looks. Make sure you view it both with and without the images downloaded, and when you are checking it you want to look out for the following things:

Does it look how I want it to?
Is it obvious what the customer needs to do next?
How did the subject line look – was it too long?

Then change your email HTML however you need to.

Story/Message

In your email marketing, there should be a flow of stories defined in your marketing promotions calendar (see Step 5). Some may be simple one-offs like "New Season Online", or "20% Off Beach Toys"; others will be a more complex series of emails like the Christmas Campaign, or Sale.

The real performance of your email marketing comes from how well your stories flow through the year, and how well each email explains its story. The story impacts on the Subject line, the Content, the Data selection, and possibly even the From Name (e.g. "Your Brand Sale").

As counter-intuitive as it sounds, not all your emails should be trying to sell. This is especially true if you are building your eCommerce business on a USP of knowledge and information or brand. Some of your emails should be purely about news or knowledge (not that they can't feature products, but the main message shouldn't be about the products), so it might be about a room a customer has created with your paints, or your clothes being worn by a key celebrity. These softer emails build up a better relationship with your customers; they make them warm to your business more and trust you more.

Of course, there is no reason why you shouldn't have an element of this in every email you send, but try sending just one non-sales email each quarter and see what impact it has.

Segmentation

Tip: See the Tip Box about Segmentation on page 72.

Segmentation is where email marketing gets really exciting: what messages do you send to what customers, when? How can you use email marketing to build your relationship with your customers and monitor how frequently they buy from you?

We discussed segmentation in detail in Step 5, and it's in email marketing that you can really make segmentation work for you. You should use your segmentation to both monitor performance and to push for better response. Every email you send should be tracked for the response it gets from each of your customer segments. You always want to know how the enquirers responded compared with how the buyers did. How did the lapsed buyers respond vs. those who bought last month? Then, even if you are just sending the same message to everyone, you can start to see how different groups behave so you know how to change things next year to increase the performance further.

Using segmentation to improve results is usually focused on campaigns designed to change customer behaviour for the better, for example:

- Welcome programmes
  To either convince enquirers to make the first purchase, or to encourage first time buyers to make the second
- Reactivation programmes:
  To get customers who haven't bought in a while to buy again

These programmes are great ways to increase the business's performance, but what's almost even better about them is that once you have got it working you can automate it.

Automating elements of your email marketing is hugely powerful and hugely efficient: you just set it up once and it works in the background, keeping the sales coming in. Not all email systems can cope with automation, so make sure you find out what you can do before you sign up.

When Doesn't Email Marketing Work?

Email Marketing doesn't work if you don't have the data. The real power of Email Marketing is when you are sending information to people who want to receive, i.e. information about your products to people who have signed up to hear from your business.

So if you don't have an email database, you need to start building one.

What to Measure in Email Marketing

EMAIL MARKETING PERFORMANCE REPORT

Subject Line	Delivered	Opened	%	Clicked	%	Orders	Value	AOV	Conversion Rate	Sales / Delivered
A	5,000	1,500	30.00%	525	35.00%	26	1,820	70	5.00%	36.4p
B	5,000	1,750	35.00%	438	25.00%	35	1,575	45	8.00%	31.5p

Below are the key metrics you need to be measuring for your email marketing; most of them are in the table above:

EMAIL MARKETING METRICS

Metric	What is it?	Benchmarks
Attempted	The number of emails you tried to send	
Delivered	The number of emails that were actually delivered	
Delivery rate	A percentage Delivered divided by Attempted	If it's not over 90%, you need to clean your data better or change your hosting and software
Opened	The number of recipients who opened your email	
Open Rate	A percentage Opened divided by Delivered	This should be over 25%. Most importantly, look at where yours usually is and take note if it changes
Clicked	The number of recipients who clicked from the email through to your website	
Click Rate	A percentage Clicked divided by Opened	This should be over 25. Most importantly, look at where yours usually is and take note if it changes
Orders	The number of orders placed as a result of the email Tracked either via your ESP or Google Analytics	
Conversion Rate	A percentage Orders divided by Clicks	This should be higher than your website's average Conversion Rate because you have targeted the email at people interested in your products.

EMAIL MARKETING METRICS (CONTINUED)

Metric	What is it?	Benchmarks
Sales	The value of the orders	
AOV	The average order value. Sales divided by Orders	Partly depends on what you are promoting in the email. But generally it should be in line with normal AOVs.
Sales per Delivered	A great way to compare the performance of emails where the list size varied. Sales divided by Delivered	After a few emails, you will see where this should be for your business – so keep an eye out for those emails/segments that under- or over-perform.
Unsubscribes	The number of recipients who unsubscribe	
Unsubscribe Rate	A percentage. Unsubscribes divided by Delivered	Every email will get unsubscribes. Normally this will be around 1%. Don't worry until it hits 2 or 3%.

If you can, it's also good to monitor the number of spam complaints you get. Plus, if you are tracking the email traffic into your Analytics system, then every three to six months have a look at how the traffic is performing: how does its behaviour differ from that of your other traffic sources?

Successful Email Marketing Checklist:

- Are you on the right software? Is your ESP doing a good job for you?
- Can you set up an SPF record?
- Select your From Name and stick with it.
- Construct a great set of stories to tell.
- Focus on telling the story well in every email.
- Get your email content structure right.
- Think about how to grow your list.
- Build your email reporting dashboard and keep looking at it.

NOTES

What are the key points from this section?

Other Notes:

WEBSITE
Visit **eCommerceMasterPlan.com** for the latest information on Email Marketing

Top Tip: Email Deliverability

The most critical thing for successful Email Marketing is getting your emails into the inbox, i.e. Email Deliverability. It is best understood by comparing email deliverability to the deliverability of physical mail (through Royal Mail):

In the offline world:
- A business gets the Royal Mail to deliver their communications to a number of recipients
- The Royal Mail aims to deliver every piece of communication for the business
- The recipient deals with the piece of communication as follows: responds/stores/ puts in the bin/ignores/contacts the business in order to be removed from future communications/registers themselves with the MPS

In the online world:
- The business gets an email sending system (could just be Outlook) to deliver their communications to a number of consumers
- The communications sent by the sending system are delivered to a number of ISPs (the bit after the @ sign: could be hotmail.com, gmail.com, myfunsite.com, etc.)
- Each ISP checks the communication and decides if they want to deliver it to their users. The checks include:
    - Looking at the content:
        - How much image is there compared to text?
        - Is it information our users want to receive?
    - Looking at where the email has come from:
        - Do we trust this sender?
        - Do others trust this sender? How have our users previously reacted to communications from this sender?
- Once the ISP has run all their checks, they do one of the following with it:
    - Deliver it to the recipient's inbox
    - Deliver it to the recipient's spam folder
    - Bin it and do not deliver it
- The recipient may interact with their emails via a number of tools. If they use the web service of their ISP (e.g. they log into Hotmail), they will see the email as supplied by the ISP. Or they may use other software to interact with their emails, such as Outlook or Thunderbird. In this case, the software will run its own set of checks on the email and decide what to do with the email: inbox or junk folder.
- If the recipient receives the piece of communication, they will deal with it as follows:
    - Respond
    - Store
    - Bin
    - Click the unsubscribe link in the email to let the business know they don't want to receive any more emails
    - Click the "SPAM" link provided by the ISP to tell the ISP they don't want to receive any more emails from the business (if too many do this, the emails won't be delivered in that ISP)

The key difference in the online world is that there are many stakeholders you can have a direct impact on if Consumer X receives your communications.

Top Tip: Find Out your SenderScore

SenderScore is a measure of email deliverability; how many spam filters you will get through. Or (roughly speaking), how likely it is that your emails will get into the inbox.

If you want to see how well your emails fare, you first need to find out the IP address from which your emails are sent. This is because your deliverability is in large part based on your IP address's reputation. Either:

- Ask your IT team.

OR

- In Outlook 2007, open the email and click on the little box at the bottom right corner of the "Options" box in the header.
- At the bottom of the pop-up is a box labelled "Internet headers". In there is the line "Received: from … ([111.11.111.11]). It is the numbers between the brackets that are your email sending IP.

Once you have got your IP address:

- Go to the HYPERLINK "https://www.senderscore.org/" SenderScore website (www.senderscore.org)
- Enter your IP in the big IP entry box
- Click "Look up"
- On the next page, a number will appear in a big red box – this is your SenderScore.

Why not check out the SenderScore of your competition while you are there.

Top Tip: SPF Records

The SPF record sits on your domain's name servers (so the same place you go to change your A records and CNAME records), and it's a text file. That means it's pretty simple to get an SPF record in place; the more complex bit is doing it right. If you are going to set up an SPF record, you need to make sure you have included EVERY location that sends email on your domain's behalf. For example, in a typical eCommerce business, this might include:

- **Your ESP for your email marketing**
- **Your Order Management System for your order despatch confirmations**
- **Your website for your order-placed emails**
- **Your head office if you use the same URL in your emails**
- **Your customer service team**

If you leave one of them out, the emails sent from that location may well not be delivered.

Steps to setting up your SPF:

- Identify everywhere your emails are sent from
- Go to HYPERLINK "http://www.openspf.org/" http://www.openspf.org/ to find out how to set up the text file
- Put it in place
- Check every location's emails are still working correctly

If any systems change, don't forget to update the SPF record.

Top Tip: Email Recruitment

We know now that buying email data is probably not a good idea. But we also know that email marketing is really effective at generating sales. So what can we do to increase the list?

The first thing to do is to make sure you are always asking for the email address, and that it is easy to give it. Just check through all the points where you interact with the customers; where can you improve email address capture? That includes stores and catalogues.

Secondly, make sure your email sign-up is obvious and compelling. Put it somewhere it's going to be seen, and make it easy to use (so ask for as little information as possible). Then test different incentives, prize draws, free downloads, free gifts: see what works best for your business.

Finally, think of where else your customers might be. What magazine or websites do they like? And would those magazines or websites be interested in running a competition for their readers? If they are, you could provide the prize and set up the entry form so that everyone who enters signs up to your emails.

When you are measuring the effectiveness of these recruitment methods, don't just look at how many email addresses you get. Keep the data from each recruitment campaign separate and see how it responds; you want good data not just any data, so the campaign that brought you data that buys is the one you want to do again.

Social Media Marketing

Social Media marketing is essential for these eCommerce Business Structures:

- Online Only
- Boutique Bricks and Clicks
- Niche PiggyBack

It is also particularly useful if your USPs are:

- Knowledge and Information – because it's a great way to show how much you know
- Customer Service – because different customers like to contact you in different ways – so you need to be there when they want to contact you.

Why Should you Use Social Media if you Are an eCommerce Business?

Social Media Marketing has an impact beyond just sales driven by social media. It will have a positive impact on your search marketing, it will activate your content marketing, and it will strengthen relationships with your customers. So there are lots of reasons to use it:

- Customers have lots of different ways to interact now; they are the ones choosing how they want to be communicated with, not the other way around. So if your customers want to communicate with you on Twitter you should join in.
- Everything you do on social media will help improve your search marketing traffic, too.
- It's a powerful way to prove how well you know your area.

However, you need to do it because you want to talk to and communicate with your customers; if you try to manipulate social media just for search marketing it won't work nearly as well as if you put the same effort into doing it "properly".

Social Media Marketing Objectives for eCommerce Businesses

Like all marketing for eCommerce, social media activity needs to bring in the sales. It will take a few months (or more) to build up a big enough follower base to get noticeable sales, so you initially also need objectives for follower growth, and the level of interaction. Not all followers are useful – you want those that are going to interact and spread the message further.

How Social Media Marketing Works

Social media is "a group of Internet-based applications that ... allow the creation and exchange of user-generated content."[3]

I like this definition because it's so simple, and social media is simple. It's just about communicating with like-minded people about things that interest you. Assuming you are interested in the products you sell, and that your customers and potential customers are also interested in those products, it should be easy. Shouldn't it?

The three reasons for not using social media that I hear most frequently from eCommerce businesses are:

1. We don't have anything to say
2. We don't have the time to do it
3. What if customers complain to us on social media?

We are going to address all of those as we go through this section, but before we get into the nitty-gritty I want to explain the core social media strategy for eCommerce.

[3] Kaplan, Andreas M. & Haenlein, Michael, 2010. "Users of the World,Unite! The challenges and opportunities of Social Media", Business Horizons 53 (1): 59–68.

No matter which social media platform you choose to use (Facebook, Twitter, Google+, or whatever launches next year), your fundamental approach should remain the same:

- Share content and engage in discussions - to build your follower base and get traffic to your website
- Follow others interested in the same topics – to build your follower base and get traffic to your website
- Tell your existing customers and lists that you are on social media so they can follow you there, too – to build your follower base and get traffic to your website
- Integrate social sharing buttons on the website – to get your website visitors doing the hard work for you by sharing your content on social media platforms (which will also build your follower base and get traffic to your website)

It really is that straightforward. You should:

- Build your follower base to increase the **Scale** of anything you post
- Create content that encourages **Engagement** with your content (that will mean your content gets seen by more people)
- Levels of Scale and Engagement will then lead to traffic to your website, and sales

So this section is all about how to approach and be successful with social media – it is not "how to do Twitter" or "how to do Google+". That is because creating your social media plan and strategy is the hard part; learning how to implement that on Facebook is the easy bit. How to build a social media plan and strategy doesn't change from year to year, but your social media tools do. A piece on how to use Twitter might not still be relevant in six months' time, but this section will be relevant in several years' time.

> **WEBSITE**
> But of course you do need the details of Twitter, Facebook, Google+, Pinterest, and whatever comes up next – so on the website we've got up-to-date information on how to use each of the tools to run your social media activity on **eCommerceMasterPlan.com**

How to Create Your Social Media Plan

> **WORKBOOK**
> To help you through this section, go to **eCommerceMasterPlan.com/Free** and download our Social Media Workbook.

There are 4 stages to creating a social media plan:

- Know your Audience
- Plan your Strategy
- Choose your Tools
- Get Going!

Stage 1: Know your Audience

The very first thing you need to research is what your audience are already doing on social media. Your audience is your customers, your potential customers, and those talking about your products. So they are the people you are going to want to be talking with on social media. To understand what they are doing on social media is not that hard, it just requires a bit of time and investigation.

First, look at your analytics. Do you already have traffic coming to your website from social media tools? If so, which ones, and how does that traffic behave?

To do this, go to the traffic sources data and do a filter search for each of the social media platforms:

- Twitter
- Facebook
- Pinterest
- LinkedIn
- plus.google
- Others you think may be relevant

Looking at this will give you a head start on working out which tools you are going to be using (if you are getting lots of visits from Twitter, then that would be a good platform to start on!).

If there is quite a bit of traffic you will also be able to see which pages of the website are being linked to – that will give you an idea of what content your audience are already sharing on social media.

Secondly, you need to take a look on the social media platforms to see how much discussion is already going on in your area. This is not as difficult as it sounds.

You need to come up with some keywords to search for. This might include:

- your brand name
- keywords that describe your sector
- product names and category names
- your competitors

Just go to each platform and search on those keywords; you'll soon find out if there are conversations already happening, and what topics they are on.

Stage 2: Plan your Strategy

In planning the strategy, we are going to look at being ready for things going wrong: your Corporate Social Media Policy, building the reporting dashboard, and planning the activity.

– Corporate Social Media Policy

A lot can go wrong in social media. So you need to be prepared for that before you start on anything else.

On the 5th February 2010, one of Vodaphone UK's customer service team tweeted on @VodaPhoneUK:

> is fed up of dirty homo's and is going after beaver
>
> VodafoneUK
> Vodafone UK

In March 2011, @ChryslerAutos tweeted

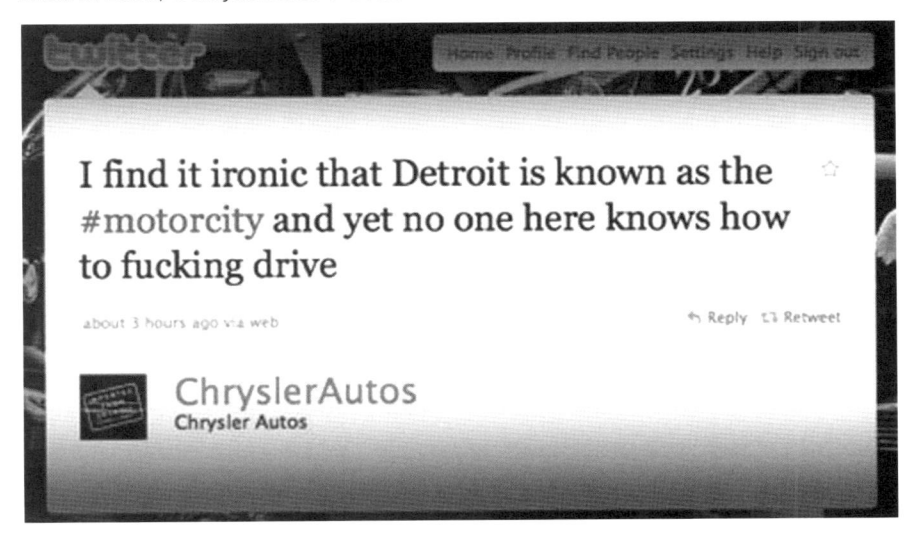

> I find it ironic that Detroit is known as the #motorcity and yet no one here knows how to fucking drive
>
> ChryslerAutos
> Chrysler Autos

Both those were one-off errors, probably people tweeting via the company Twitter rather than a different one. They were simple errors of human judgement.

The retailer Kenneth Cole couldn't use that excuse in February 2011, when they used the #Cairo to promote their new spring collection, even customising the short URL to include Cairo!

> Millions are in uproar in #Cairo. Rumor is they heard our new spring collection is now available online at http://bit.ly/KCairo -KC
> less than a minute ago via Twitter for BlackBerry®
>
> **KC** **Kenneth Cole**
> KennethCole

The first two examples highlight the inherent danger of social media communication. Messages are short, conversations need to flow, and activity is done quickly. You can't proof every social media message like you would an advertising campaign.

The impact of all three was huge, because these messages got retweeted and spread like wildfire through the internet. For Kenneth Cole, it was particularly bad as this is the first time many people had ever heard of them. With social media you don't have control over your content. You won't find any of these tweets on the accounts they were originally tweeted on – all were deleted very quickly. But by that point they had already been re-tweeted, so the content was unstoppable.

Although these errors spread very far, very fast, they die out quite quickly when apologies are swiftly issued. It's also possible to put in place guidelines and training to minimise the likelihood of it happening. In creating your social media corporate guidelines, you need to create and implement the following:

- A disaster recovery plan – how will you deal with an issue such as the above if it happens? This should include steps such as deleting the content, issuing an apology, investigating quickly, and dealing with the cause of the problem.
- Social Media HR policy, to enable you to take swift action when necessary.
- Social Media Usage Policy – that everyone is familiar with and obeys. This needs to be simple and easy to understand, but cover the basics like "do not use personal social media accounts at the same time as the company account". (See the Top Tip on page 123 for some examples.)

– Objectives and Reporting Dashboard

As ever, before doing any marketing you need to work out what your objectives are. We have already discussed that in some detail at the start of the section, plus at the end you will find a guide to social media reporting.

Unlike most of the marketing we are discussing in this book, one of your key objectives with social media needs to be to keep creating the content and consistently engaging with people on social media. The key to success is to keep communicating.

Building Engagement is what will drive people to the website, and ultimately to buy.

– Activity Plan

We have now got the corporate social media policies in place, and our objectives and reporting sorted out. So next we need to work out what we're actually going to do!

There are two parts to the activity plan. The first is to decide how the social media will be promoted by the rest of our marketing, and the second is to work out what you are going to be talking about, and who is going to be talking about it.

How do you promote the social media with the rest of your marketing? Essentially you are going to put links to your social media activity on all your customer touch points.

With your online marketing, you should add active buttons wherever you can. Along with the offline marketing activity, you should include "Find us on …" text and logos that make it easy for people to find and follow you on social media.

Active buttons are buttons that don't just link someone to your social media pages; when clicked on, that person (if they are logged into their social media profile) will be added as a follower. You can download these buttons from each tool then get your website builder or email coder to add each piece of code to your online marketing. Or you can use a tool like Add This, who will give you one set of code that will add all your social media buttons. Active buttons come in lots of shapes and sizes, so have a look at what is available on your chosen social media and implement the right one for you. Just make sure you put it in place, as it's a great way to increase your number of followers.

All of that is pretty much a one-off task that, once in place and part of your processes, you don't need to worry too much about. Your communications are where you are going to be spending your time and effort.

Building the activity plan

Firstly, you need to work out what content you have got that you can share on social media. This is the process we detailed at the start of Section 2 when we were creating our content marketing plans. Into this, you should integrate the information you found when researching what your audience are talking about already on social media.

The content you have on your website will be at the heart of your social media activity, not least because your end goal is to get people to the website, and to buy.

On top of this, though, you want to be interacting with other people. This interaction will be in the form of conversations you start, and conversations you join. This activity will build Engagement, and Engagement is what will drive your traffic.

To find conversations you want to join in you need to keep an eye on what is happening on your social media profiles; once you reach a certain scale of followers, you will find people start contacting you with questions and just to share information. This content needs to be interacted with fairly quickly, within 24 hours or so at most. But not all conversations you want to be part of will come to you: you also want to go out and find conversations to join.

When researching the audience, you identified a number of keywords to search on: these are your starting point for finding conversations to join. Every day or so (depending on the volume of content), you should be checking these searches to find conversations to join in with. Look out especially for people who are already talking about you!

So, finding conversations to join in is pretty easy. Well, so is creating conversations! Sharing the content on the website will create some of these, but you want to be more proactive than that. You need to create social media campaigns.

A social media campaign is a series of communications on the same topic, which aim to provoke debate. They can be very simple, such as "Top 10 British Authors", or very complex, such as "Design the cover of our new catalogue to win one of everything in it".

> **WEBSITE**
> You can find lots of examples of great social media campaigns on the website **eCommerceMasterPlan.com**

Initially you should be aiming for a campaign at least every month, and try different types of campaigns. Then you will learn quickly what works best; what gets the most engagement. The campaigns can run across all your social media, or just one platform. The best campaigns are ones that create new campaigns; so you might do a campaign that's a survey or poll, then you can publish the results (providing content and PR), and ask for comments on the results, and 12 months later you can re-run it to see what has changed.

Stage 3: Choose your Tools

Now you should have LOADS of ideas of what you want to do in your social media, and be itching to get going.

Before you can do that, though, you need to choose which social media platforms you are going to use, and then implement the tools you are going to use to make your social media activity efficient and effective.

There are hundreds of social media tools, from Facebook and Twitter to Pinterest and Stumbleupon. You need to choose which you are going to use, and when – you don't have to start them all at once. The research we did into where your audience is should make that decision pretty easy, but you also need to bear in mind how popular each tool is. As I'm writing this, Twitter and Facebook are big and well-established, but Google+ and Pinterest are gaining ground fast. However, that might not be the case when you come to choose your social media platforms.

> **WEBSITE**
> You will find up-to-date statistics on each of the main social media engines on the website **eCommerceMasterPlan.com** to help you make your decision.

You may decide that you want to at least establish a profile on several sites, but concentrate your efforts on one initially; that can be a great way to go as you will get real feedback on how quickly each grows for you.

Now you know what platforms you are going to use you are almost ready to start. But first we need to get the tools in place that are going to make your social media activity efficient and effective; to put it simply, save you time and enable you to do more.

Social Media Marketing | 117

This is the secret of social media. As we worked through the content you were probably thinking "this is going to take me hours, every week!" or "I know I'm going to forget to do it some days". Well, it's not going to take you as much time as you think, and it doesn't matter if you forget some days.

There are thousands of tools out there that will help you manage your social media activity and help you do things like:

- Schedule the activity, so you can set up all the communication for your campaign in one go.
- Find people to follow who are interested in the same things as you.
- Run competitions.
- Encourage email sign-ups.
- Automatically post content as you create it – yes, your blog posts can be set up to be posted automatically on to all your social media. The same can be done with images and videos, too.
- Run your searches.
- Let you know when there is something you need to respond to.
- Report.

Plus there are lots of options for each one: some are free, some you pay for, but spending a little time now finding the right ones for you and putting them in place will save you days of effort later and make all your efforts more effective.

By automating some content, you can afford to forget one day, because communications will be happening anyway. By scheduling a campaign in one go, it will be more cohesive and therefore more powerful.

WEBSITE
On the website you will find mind maps of the key tools available for the social media engines. Each map is divided into the type of activity you'll want to do, and links either to the tool itself or a review with more information: eCommerceMasterPlan.com

Stage 4: Get Going!

You should now have a pretty solid social media plan, so you can start your activity.

Don't forget to check the results, and change your strategy as you need to; there's always things changing in social media so you need to be ready to drop tactics that aren't working any more, and embrace new opportunities.

Customer Service on Social Media

Sooner or later your social media activity will attract customer service queries, so you need to be ready for that. Here are a few handy tips to make sure you are prepared:

- Involve the Customer Service team from the start – make sure they understand how you are going to be using the social media, and listen to what they think about how customers will respond.
- Make sure they are ready to get involved as soon as you get customer queries coming in. Include them in the training process.
- It is fine to ask a customer on social media to email more details to your Customer Services so you can deal with the issue more effectively.
- Try to get back to any Customer Service comments within a few working hours.
- Take a look at your existing Customer Service response times – if you are not getting back to emails within 24 hours, you are likely to get lots on social media. So try and speed up existing response times so that customers don't have to resort to social media.

One of our clients launched a competition on Facebook but hadn't briefed the store staff, so the first few comments were complaints that they couldn't enter! By including them from the start you can avoid such incidents.

One Piece of Social Media that EVERY eCommerce Business Should Embrace: Share buttons

Share buttons are the buttons you see on each page of a website that enable visitors to easily share the content on social media:

SHARE BUTTONS

Share this: Share +1 0   Tweet 1   Facebook   Email
Share

On an eCommerce site, Share buttons should be on every product page, fairly prominently. By putting them on the page you are making, it becomes really easy for customers to share the great products they are finding on your website with others. That is great news for you because:

- it is social media activity you don't have to start
- It gives you a conversation to join in – you can thank them for tweeting your products
- it helps you get more search traffic (see Section 2, page 145)

Getting the buttons in place is pretty easy (just like the Like/Follow buttons that get people to like your social media profiles). Either you can go to each social media tool and access their code and put that in place, or you can use a tool like AddThis to gather all the code into one for you. Then just get it added to the product page template, and you are all set.

When Doesn't Social Media Work?

Social media doesn't work if you haven't got anything to say. There is nothing more detrimental to a customer's perception than a dormant, unloved social media profile. So if you are not going to commit to engaging in the conversation, don't start it.

As well as having something to say, in eCommerce you also need to have the Customer Service team on board; sooner or later you will get customer queries coming through, so make sure you are ready.

There are also a few regulated industries where it's hard to engage in Social Media because there are huge restrictions on what you can and can't say in your marketing.

What to Measure in Social Media Marketing

There is a wealth of statistics available in social media. I have found the following structure the easiest way to compare performance across channels and keep the data to a manageable level. Essentially you need at least one of each of these types of metric for each social media channel you are engaged with:

- Productivity
- Engagement
- Scale
- Activity

For example:

KEY METRICS BY SOCIAL MEDIA PLATFORM

	Twitter	Facebook	Pinterest	Google+
Productivity		Visits to your website Sales		
Engagement	Retweets Mentions Tweets about you	Comments on content Likes of content	Pins of your images Likes of images	+1s of content Comments Hangouts
Scale	Followers	Page Likes	Board Followers	Page Followers
Activity	Number of tweets How many following	Content put up Conversations engaged in	Items pinned Items Liked Conversations engaged in	Content put up Hangouts engaged in Size of circles

SOCIAL MEDIA MARKETING METRICS

Metric	What is it?	Benchmarks
Productivity	A way of tracking the actual impact of your social media activity Sales and website visits	Initially you will find you get very little productivity response to your social media activity, but as your Scale and Engagement builds, you will be able to compare this with previous months and other channels
Engagement	How much your customers engage with you on social media You'll find this is the number that influences sales	As you grow your social media activity, you will be creating your own set of benchmarks for how you expect engagement to function
Scale	The size of your social media audience You need some volume here in order to drive enough Engagement to drive enough Productivity	You want this to keep growing – but only with quality followers If they are not engaging with you, there is no point in having them
Activity	What did you do? You need to track what you did in order to see how that increases Scale and Engagement	

Social media is hard to track – not all the numbers we need are easily available. With a lot of them you can only get numbers by noting them down on the day, so you need to make sure you keep up to date with compiling your social media performance.

There are a number of social media reporting tools; some paid, some free. I haven't yet found one at a reasonable price that gives me what I want in my reporting, but as soon as I do find one, I will be writing about it at eCommerceMasterPlan.com! In the meantime, I have put some mindmaps of useful social media tools, including reporting tools, on the website.

Successful Social Media Marketing Checklist

- Have you selected the right social media platforms? (Twitter, Facebook, etc.)
- Have you got your automated activity in place?
- Have you got the tools set up to make it easy for you to run?
- Is the reporting dashboard ready?
- Do you know what you are going to be communicating about for the next few months?
- Is your customer services team ready to go?
- Have you worked out a corporate social media strategy?

NOTES

What are the key points from this section?

Other Notes:

WEBSITE
Visit **eCommerceMasterPlan.com** for the latest information on the key social media tools, including case studies of what is working for other eCommerce businesses, and guides on setting up your social media tools.

Top Tip: Social Media Glossary

Social media seems more complex than it is because of all the jargon. Hopefully this social media glossary will help a bit:

Twitter:
- Followers – twitter users who are signed up to read your tweets.
- Tweets – 140-character messages you post on your Twitter account (these can include links).
- Retweet – when you post something someone else has tweeted already – it shows in a tweet as "RT".
- Hash tags – the # sign is used to prefix certain topics e.g. #xmas or #generalelection. This is useful if you are part of a group discussing a certain topic, and it makes events easier to follow via Twitter Search.
- @Reply – a tweet sent direct to another twitter user, for when you are having a one-to-one conversation.
- DM – a direct message sent from one user to another that cannot be seen by other users.
- FF – Follow Friday. On a Friday, users often use the hash tag #FF and suggest a list of people worth following.

Facebook:
- Facebook Profile – the identity for individuals on Facebook.
- Facebook Page – the identify for businesses on Facebook.
- Status Update – an update provided by a Page or Profile. Might be a link, text, image or video.
- Followers – the people who have liked your Facebook Page.
- Timeline – the new (2012) format for Facebook Pages and Profiles. It shows a big image at the top and updates laid out like a timeline down the page.
- Like button – the key to Facebook success for businesses – you want people to "Like" your Facebook Page, AND to "Like" your other online content.
- Poke – the old-school way to attract people's attention on Facebook. It is not used so much now.
- News Feed – the centre of your Facebook universe. This is where you see what's happening with everyone else.
- EdgeRank – the algorithm that decides what each person sees on their News Feed. The better you do, the more engagement you will have.
- Edge – anything that happens on Facebook: a status update, liking a status update, uploading an image, becoming friends with someone. These are the things that Facebook prioritises with the EdgeRank.

LinkedIn:
- Connection – someone you are linked to (all connections are two-way; you both need to want to connect to each other).
- Company Page – the profile of a company, where you can find out information about their staff, what they do, and other information.
- Groups – the centre of activity on LinkedIn; you can join many groups and contribute to the debate. There are groups on thousands of different subjects.
- LinkedIn Today – their news service. This compiles information they believe will be useful for you (based on who you are connected to).
- Answers – the Q&A area of LinkedIn. Help someone out by answering a question, or get help by posting one.

Pinterest:
- Pins – images that have been "pinned" to boards.
- Boards – online pin boards where you "pin" images you like. You can have lots of boards, so group images into themes.
- Pin It button – the button a user adds to their browser bookmarks to pin any image they find online.
- Repin – add an image you find on Pinterest to one of your boards.
- Like – Like an image you find on Pinterest.
- Follow – follow a board or a person on Pinterest.

Google+:
- Profile – the identity for individuals on Google+.
- Page or Local – the identity for businesses on Google+.
- Posts – updates provided by a Page or Profile; it might be a link, text, image or video.
- Circles – a way to group together people and pages you want to connect with.
- Hangouts – have a video chat with up to nine people.

WEBSITE
Find our latest social media glossary at
eCommerceMasterPlan.com

Top Tip: Social Media Usage Policies

Social Media Usage policies come in *many* shapes and sizes. Here are some examples:
- **Zappos.com** simply state: be real and use your best judgement
- **eConsultancy** have two versions: the short (be nice, don't tell lies, don't feed the trolls) and the full version, which is:
1. Listen closely. That's what your ears are for.
2. Respond to questions/queries/concerns in a timely fashion.
3. When you respond, remember that you are a human, not a 'PRbot'. A little personality is more than OK.
4. Have a thick skin and take all criticism on the chin (but stick up for yourself where necessary).
5. Learn the difference between cheekiness and spaminess. Kiss the former, kill the latter.
6. Coordination and consistency (of messaging) is important. Talk among yourselves.
7. Raise flags internally, as and when appropriate.
8. Denial, wool-pulling and hole-digging is bad. Admitting mistakes and saying sorry is good (relatively speaking).
9. Always pause for a moment in private before you reply in public.
10. Be responsible.

- **IBM** state:
1. Don't pick fights; be the first to correct your own mistakes, and don't alter previous posts without indicating that you have done so.
2. Try to add value. Provide worthwhile information and perspective. IBM's brand is best represented by its people, and what you publish may reflect on IBM's brand.
3. Speak in the first person. Use your own voice. Bring your own personality to the forefront. Say what is on your mind.

- **BBC** say:
1. With conversations, participate online. Don't "broadcast" messages to users.
2. In moderation, we only police where we have to. We trust our users where we don't.
3. Tone of voice: we should be sensitive to the expectations of existing users of the specific site. If we add a BBC presence, we are joining their site rather than the opposite. Users are likely to feel that they already have a significant stake in it. When adding an informal BBC presence, we should "go with the grain" and be sensitive to user customs and conventions, to avoid giving the impression that the BBC is imposing itself on them and their space.

- **INTEL** (the short version) advise:
Always pause and think before posting.
Perception is reality.
It is a conversation.

Top Tip: Tracking Social Media Traffic to your Website

The traffic sent to your website by social media will be reported in your analytics as various sources. Some will be simply from the URL of the tool (e.g. Twitter.com), and some will come in tagged as the tool you are using (e.g. Twitter /Twitterfeed).

This makes reporting on the impact of social media quite tricky – not least in Google Analytics, because their "Social Media" tool is currently only picking up the raw URL data, not traffic from links that have tagging on them. So, when you are reporting on the traffic and sales impact, make sure you are gathering all the sources together. Also, to track the performance of individual campaigns, you may want to tag the links you are putting in that campaign so you can see them separately in Google Analytics, too.

You will find more on tagging links in Step 3.

Brand Awareness Marketing

Building Brand Awareness is essential for these eCommerce Business Structures:

- Online Only
- Big Bricks and Clicks
- Niche PiggyBack
- Full Multichannel

It is also particularly useful if your USP is:

- Brand – if your USP is your brand then you must build that brand.
- Customer Service – if you are building a reputation for great customer service that sits very well with building brand awareness.
- Knowledge and information – this is both a way to build brand awareness and something to base that brand on

Why should you Build Brand Awareness if you are an eCommerce Business?

The more aware a potential customer is of your business, the more likely they are to buy from you. Customer awareness is a way to remove barriers to conversion (see Part 2).
If what they know about your business is good, they are far more likely to buy; if what they know about your business is consistent – again, they are far more likely to buy.

Building brand awareness is about making sure your target consumers know about your business, AND that the impression they have is the right one: the one you want them to have.

So you should be building brand awareness because:

- The more aware your target customers are of your brand, the easier it will be convince them to buy.
- If your customers feel strongly about your brand, they are more likely to forgive you when mistakes happen. So it builds loyalty.
- It also improves the response of all your marketing activity – people become pre-disposed to your marketing before they have even realised what you are selling this time.

Brand Awareness Objectives for eCommerce Businesses

It is very hard to measure the impact of brand awareness building activity. That means it is pretty difficult to set objectives.
When I worked at Barclays, brand awareness was measured on a "warmth" scale (from 0–100), so every month or so a survey was done to see how "warmly" consumers felt about Barclays. Before the bank started actively tracking this warmth scale, a management consultancy had worked out that if "warmth" could be increased by 1 point it would be the equivalent of an extra several 100,000 on the bottom line. Barclays spent a vast sum of money on coming up with the formulas and tracking the results. That is beyond most eCommerce businesses, but it doesn't mean that there shouldn't be brand awareness objectives.

Every business has the sales objective of an increase in overall sales. If you get the branding right and consistent across all your marketing, everything should improve (response rates, AOV, customer retention, conversion rate, and more). If, right now, you don't have a strong brand, it will take months (if not years) for you to see the impact of the brand awareness activity.

How Building Brand Awareness Works

Traditionally brand awareness has been left to the PR department, but now it's more complex. It is more complex both because there are now so many more ways to go about it (from events, to social media, to press, to everything in between), and because you have to live up to what you say your brand is.

To build brand awareness you need to engage in three areas:

- Have a clear brand, and be clear on what it stands for
- Consistently deliver that brand
- Do activity 'above the parapet' that will put your brand in front of lots of people

In this section, we are going to run through each of these areas in turn.

> **WORKBOOK**
> Build your brand awareness building plan more successfully by going to the website and downloading the Brand Awareness Workbook from here: **eCommerceMasterPlan.com/Free**

Identifying Your Brand and What it Stands For

Your brand is much more than just a logo. It is the identity that customers, and future customers, engage with and believe in. So you want them to trust it and to feel an affinity with it. It will also overlap a lot with your USP, as your USP is what your company should pride itself on.

Whatever stage your business is at, you probably already have a good idea of what your brand is. So this step really is about identifying that brand, not creating it.

To identify it, you need to find out what everyone thinks it is. So gather the thoughts of your team in answer to the following questions. (You might want to do this via a meeting, an email, or survey, or even an evening down the pub – it depends on the size of your team!)

- What is [company name]?
- What do customers think when they think of [company name]?
- What do we want customers to think of when they think of us?
- Who are we?
- What do we do?
- What do we stand for?

You may also find it useful to ask the same questions of people outside your business: your friends, or key suppliers.

You will get very different answers to all those questions; but you will also see some real themes emerging. Hopefully the themes are ones you want your brand to stand for; then it's going to be much easier to implement.

Either by yourself, or with your management team, you then need to crystallize the information you have gathered and pull it all together into a coherent statement about what the brand is and what it stands for.

Once you have worked out what your brand stands for, you need to create:

- A logo
- A voice/brand statement: what does the brand (your company) stand for? It should be distilled to a page or two of copy.
- A set of brand guidelines: how can the logo be used, what fonts do you use, colours, etc.?

Consistency: Living up to your brand

Now you have got your brand clearly outlined, you need to make sure that your whole business reflects that brand. Right from the marketing you send out, to the products, and to the packaging they arrive to your customer in.

If your brand is about luxury, you need to be sending out your products in quality packaging – not just stuffed in a jiffy bag! If you brand is about the environment, you should be minimising your packaging as much as possible. If you are all about customer service, then why do you not take calls on a Sunday? The more you explore the brand, the more you will realise how important it is to consistently reflect it in everything the business does.

The first thing you need to do is to look at every touch point the customer has with you: how well does every step line up with the brand? Identify everything you are doing that is not in line with your brand, and change it. You will also find lots of activity that is not quite as consistent as it could be: this also will need to be improved.

Of course, you can't do all this overnight, so you need to plan how everything is going to be made consistent with the brand. A lot of this will rely on people, so as part of this you must make sure everyone understands the brand, why it is important, and how what they do day to day can affect it.

Your brand is only as good as your last interaction with a customer, so everything needs to be on brand, every time. To truly make that happen, you can't only focus on getting the customer-facing activity on-brand. Everything the business does needs to be on-brand. For example, if you are all about customer service yet your own employees feel like they are treated badly, then you need to improve your HR processes. If you are a luxury brand and your team have to drink cheap instant coffee you should probably install a good coffee machine.

It is well worth spending time and money on getting everything you do consistent with your brand; this is the activity that will make it obvious what you stand for, without you having to do endless PR campaigns. It will be obvious what you stand for because it's what you do day in day out.

Taking your Brand above the Parapet to Build Awareness

Simply making your brand consistent in the business will build awareness on its own; staff and customers will talk about the experience they have had and how it appealed to them. Once you are thoroughly living up to your brand, you can take it above the parapet to accelerate how quickly people become aware of your brand and company.

By this point, you are already making your brand clear in all your marketing activity – so there's already quite a bit of brand awareness being built. But there is more you can do to accelerate the process. What you can do depends on your brand itself, because what you do needs to fit with it.

If you are all about the lowest prices in vitamins, then hiring a cruise ship for a week for your 100 best customers, suppliers, and journalists would be an odd thing to do. Proving you are the best value and running a PR campaign on that wouldn't be an odd thing to do, nor would sponsoring some amateur sports teams.

The aim of any above-the-parapet activity you plan to do is to generate conversations about your business: conversations that reinforce your brand and that people will remember. So you need to choose your methods and content carefully; think through any potential issues that might arise through the message getting confused.

Common brand awareness-raising tactics include:

- Press Releases and other PR activity
- Blogger liaison – building relationships with influential bloggers in your marketplace
- Social media
- Surveys and opinion polls
- Events – both organised events and flash-mob style spontaneous events
- Sponsorship
- Creating a 'National Day of X'

In common with all marketing, some of these are very cheap while others can be hugely expensive. But with social media now having such an impact on the news, it can be quite easy to come up with simple, effective, and cheap ways to build your brand.

It is time for another brainstorm to work out what you should do. Now your team are clear on what the brand stands for, and have seen how focusing on it has changed the business, it's time to get together and see what ideas you can come up with – from the big and crazy to the small and simple. Make a note of all the ideas, and pick one of the simpler ones to start with!

When Doesn't Building Brand Awareness Work?

Every eCommerce business will benefit from getting brand consistency across their customer interactions. So no eCommerce business should entirely ignore brand awareness, but you should be doing what fits your market and business size. If you are an Etsy seller, going to a craft show or getting featured in an Etsy email are great ideas, but running a billboard campaign less so.

Not all eCommerce businesses will benefit from going beyond that in building brand awareness. Smaller businesses selling price-sensitive products are much less likely to find it worthwhile; so if you are selling commodity electronics, customers are going to buy from you because you've got that specific camera at the best price. Saying that, if you are in that marketplace and you want to get serious growth, then you are going to reach a point where you need to keep customers buying from you, and at that point brand awareness will become important.

How to Measure Brand Awareness

Measuring brand awareness is not easy. As we discussed above, it ultimately will be judged a success or not if your sales and overall performance increases.

You should be looking at trends in all statistics you are measuring, and those should be improving if you are brand awareness is working. In addition, something I have always found useful to do is gather some data via a customer survey. Asking a mix of quantitive and qualitative questions should give you an idea of how customers feel about businesses. I would run questions similar to the following ones every six months, collecting the responses both of website visitors and buyers:

- How likely are you to recommend [business name] to others?
  (On a scale of 1 to 4.)
- If you could change one thing about [business name] what would it be?
  (Open response.)
- What is your favourite thing about [business name]?
  (Open Response.)
- What other stores/websites/catalogues do you buy products like ours from? (Initially you will have an open box here, but after the first few surveys you will be able to change that to a series of tick boxes with an "Other" box included.)

The last question is particularly useful because it helps you work out which brands you are up against, so you can look at how they are positioning themselves and make sure you are at least one step ahead.

Successful Brand Awareness Checklist

- Really understand the brand you are promoting.
- Make sure everything the business does fits with the brand – everything!
- All promotional activity and activity to build brand awareness should fit with the brand, too.
- Track the impact on how aware people are of you, but also the impact on bottom line sales.

NOTES

What are the key points from this section?

Other Notes:

WEBSITE
Visit **eCommerceMasterPlan.com** for more information on how eCommerce businesses are building their brands.

Offline Marketing

Offline marketing is essential for these eCommerce Business Structures:

- Mail Order
- Big Bricks and Clicks
- Boutique Bricks and Clicks
- Full Multichannel

It is also particularly useful if your USP is:

- Brand – to build a brand you need to build awareness, and offline marketing can give you much greater visibility than online alone.

Why Should you use Offline Marketing if you are an eCommerce Business?

Offline marketing is usually used by eCommerce businesses to provide something they can't get online. Generally it is linked to scale: getting in front of more people, getting hold of a bigger list, increasing response. So as well as providing something you can't get with online marketing, it can also be a way to accelerate the growth of your business. Offline marketing has the following benefits:

- It's a more mature marketplace; it's been around longer, and there are mapped-out ways to do things. So it can be very straightforward to do.
- The maturity of the market means there is more volume to be had. For example, we discussed in Section 2 (Email Marketing) that renting email data is a bad idea, because good quality lists don't exist. That is not the case with offline data – there are hundreds of great sources of quality, responsive mailing data that will perform for you.
- Response rates with offline direct marketing are greater than with online direct marketing.
- Visibility is much greater offline than online – billboards and TV and Radio hit many more people than online advertising, and get better engagement.

Offline Marketing Objectives for eCommerce Businesses

Offline marketing activity should be focused on hitting your big objective: Sales.

You might, however, want to focus on targets that are a step away from profit and sales, such as building a list, or brand awareness.

Offline marketing (broadly) has a slower impact than online marketing, so it takes longer to optimise it. You may be able to optimise your PPC Campaigns within six months, but with your postal mailings it will take a year or more to optimise your choice of lists. It also tends to cost a lot more than online marketing (in actual spend, if not in ROI), and as the response comes in slower, you have to be able to risk more with Offline Marketing.

How Offline Marketing Works

Offline marketing could simply be any marketing you do that isn't on your website or online. So it has a lot of overlap with the brand awareness activity we discussed in the last section. Here, we are going to focus the definition a little more, to be: marketing which happens offline that is intended to directly drive sales, not just awareness.

In this case Offline Marketing works by driving customers to visit your website (or shop, or phone you) and order. This broadly falls into three categories:

- **Direct Marketing**
  Where you select potential customers to target, usually by buying a list of data and mailing them something in the post.

- **Shops and Shows**
  Literally, taking your products out to the customers. That could be in your shop, or having a stand at a show of some sort.
- **Advertising**
  Where you select potential customers by demographic and interests, and put advertising in places likely to appeal to people of that segment. Usually this would be advertising in newspapers and magazines, but it could include billboards, TV or radio.

Direct marketing

Direct Mail is a hugely powerful way to recruit customers and generate sales. Response rates are much better than with most forms of online marketing: usually 1% or higher, even for cold mailings. You can actually buy data that is good quality and well-targeted, but it requires a lot of cash upfront to do it.

> **WORKBOOK**
> Download our Direct Mailing Workbook from the website now to help you build your direct mail campaign: **ecommerceMasterPlan.com/free**

A pack for direct mail could be anything from a simple postcard to a several hundred-page catalogue. Costs and responses differ massively depending on what format you choose to go with. If you have never done any volume direct mail before, I strongly recommend you get someone involved who has experience in this area as they will be able to improve your performance and save you a lot of money and effort along the way. Direct mail is a very mature tactic, so there are lots of tips and tricks that could save you a packet.

Once you have decided on your mailing format you need to start creating your campaign. You want to start this at least a few months before you want to post it.

Find the data

If you don't have anyone to send your mailing to, it's not going to work! So before committing to any other costs you should make sure you can get enough quality data to make the activity hit your targets.

Every mailing will probably include a mix of data you already have and cold data that you have bought or swapped, so in creating your data plan you should consider the following:

- What data do you already have that's bought from you?
- What data do you have that hasn't been previously bought from you (your enquirers)?
- Would any of your target partners (see page 183) be willing to swap data with you?
- Would any of your target partners be willing to rent you data?
- Speak to a list broker. If you explain who you are targeting, they will provide you with a list of suggestions for data you could swap or buy.
- Speak to the data cooperatives. These are businesses who compile vast databases from which they can create a list of the type of customers you want for you – usually based on geo-demographic profiling tools.

Remember that all your mailings should have elements of data testing in them. So even if one of the possible cold data sources has a possible 100,000 you could mail, don't. Just test 10–20,000 sources then roll out to the rest in your next mailing if it's successful.

Once you know you can get the data and how many you are going to be mailing, you can start the design process.

Design it

Depending on the size of the mailing piece, this could be a short or a very long process. Assuming you are going to feature products in the mailing piece, you will need to go through the following stages:

- Selection – choose the products you are going to feature
- Create an outline – what products on which pages (and other content)
- Photograph all the products
- Write all the copy
- Start designing
- Several rounds of proofing and sign off
- Then send it to the repro house; they will make sure the colours are right. It is very important when you are aiming to get people to buy products that the products looks like they do in the pictures.
- Finally prepare the designs for the printers

Don't forget the response mechanisms and call to actions:

- Do tell them to buy/visit the website
- Include the URL
- Include the phone number
- Include your social media locations

Paper, Print, Bind

In order to turn your designs into reality you need to source the paper, organise the printers, and if you have multiple pages get the whole thing bound together. Your printers may be able to do all three stages, but often you will need to use a separate binding house – so make sure you have got the number of a good courier in case you need them.

You will also be given the opportunity to proof your mailing on press. If you have high production values, then this is a really important step to commit to. This is your opportunity to make sure the mailing looks just right.

Back when I looked after mailing campaigns for Past Times, we produced a Christmas-themed, self-sealed mailing piece that went out to about 100,000 people, to encourage them to visit their local store in the run-up to Christmas. It was a really clever piece, with the map and address of the local store printed in it, and it did drive a great response: a response that would probably have been better if one of us had gone to proof it on press and realised that the colour mix on the red was wrong. As it was, we posted 100,000 pink Christmas mailings to our customers. Make sure you don't make that mistake!

Posting and Mailing

Once your mailing piece is ready you will need to get it into the post.

Over the last few years, this has got much more complex. It used to be that you had to use Royal Mail (which was complex enough), but now there are lots of different routes into the postal system.

The biggest determinant of how much you pay in postage is the size and weight of the mailing piece. Once that is set, though, there is more you can do to further reduce the costs.

- If you are not in a hurry for your mailing to land, you can send it even slower than 2nd class, usually landing within seven days.
- If you can get your mailing data right you can also prepare it for the postal service by putting it in the right order – that's called MailSort or WalkSort. This means it is easier for the Royal Mail to process, so again you'll pay less.

In addition to the postage, you'll also need to pay a mailing house to put the mail in the post (and polywrap it if you need that done). That can sometimes be done by your printers, too.

It's worth talking to a mailing house, or postage specialist, early in the process to make sure you get the best deal and service possible. They will be able to help you get the mailing piece right for the best deal.

Shops and Shows

Having a shop or running a stand at shows are great ways to recruit new customers. The Number One aim of either is to sell product there and then, but you should also be aiming to gather customer details (to mail them and email them), and make them aware of the website.

You should have your website address clearly on anything they leave with – bag, receipt, flyer, etc. The website address should also be clearly visible to anyone in the shop or walking past; put it on the shop windows and any other big wall spaces you have.

Having a sign-up competition to gather details can work really well, too – just a postcard sized form for people to fill in with a prize of gift vouchers can generate a lot of extra customer data. Always ask for a customer's email address and postal address if you are sending out mailings, too. Less than 10% of people who come into your shop or stall will buy – so try and at least get the data of the others.

Advertising

Billboards, TV, and Radio are more about building brand awareness than driving a direct sales response; they can also be very expensive and are hard to optimise. So I'm going to concentrate on the forms of advertising that can drive a direct response:

- Off-the-page advertising
- Inserts

Both these methods are focused on print journalism, which is great because it means you can easily target the right type of people. When you run a customer survey, ask them which magazines and newspapers they read and that will give you your list of titles to advertise in.

Both these methods have been used for decades by the mail order industry to recruit new customers, and they are still working today.

Off-the-page adverts are the ones you see in the back of every section of every weekend paper, usually focused on an offer for one particular product, with an order form at the bottom of the page. If you are going down this route, engage a design agency that specialises in this type of advert; it is a science to get it right and you will keep changing the advert to make sure the response is just right.

If you want to get serious with Off-the-page, then have your adverts ready and call the papers on a Friday to see what last-minute space they have. You can usually snap that up at a huge discount.

Done well, off-the-page advertising can provide you with a customer recruitment vehicle that makes a profit!

If you are producing a catalogue or a flyer, you should test inserting the catalogue in newspapers and magazines. It's much cheaper than cold mailing because you don't have the postage costs to worry about, but response rates tend to be lower. Find the right publication to insert into, though, and you'll find a great way to recruit new customers.

When Doesn't Offline Marketing Work?

As you have seen in this section, there are many forms of offline marketing. I struggle to think of any business that wouldn't benefit from mailing its existing customers – even if it's just a postcard to tell them the sale is on.

Offline marketing requires a different set of skills to online marketing, and behaves very differently financially – you make the investment upfront and once the activity's gone out the door there is nothing you can do to affect it. So you need to be ready for that, too.

Don't embark on offline marketing until your business is ready; the systems can cope with it, and you have a way to get the expertise to make it work first time.

What to Measure in Offline Marketing

As I wrote at the start of the section, offline marketing is usually done to build sales (via Direct Activity), or to build awareness (via Advertising). Those need to be tracked differently. For some activity, you'll want to track it in both ways.

DIRECT ACTIVITY PERFORMANCE REPORT

Activity	Distributed	Cost	Cost per Item	Orders	Value	AOV	Response Rate	Cost/Profit per Order
Mailing to List A	5,000	7,000	1.4	51	3,570	70	1.00%	-67.25
Mailing to List B	5,000	5,000	1	102	6,120	60	2.00%	1.17
Insert in Magazine A	5,000	3,000	0.6	25	1,250	50	0.50%	-70

ADVERTISING ACTIVITY PERFORMANCE REPORT

Activity	Impressions	Cost	Cost per 1000 Impressions	Brand Recall	Sign-ups Rate	Response
Radio	5,000,000	7,000	1.4	51.00%	3,000	0.06%
Billboards	50,000	5,000	100	10.00%	500	1.00%
Feature in Magazine	500,000	3,000	6	60.00%	1,000	0.20%

Below are the key metrics you need to be measuring; most are in the tables above:

OFFLINE MARKETING METRICS

Metric	What is it?	Benchmarks
Distributed	The number of items you have distributed in that way. Catalogues or direct mail sent, copies of the magazine, etc.	
Cost	How much it costs. Remember to include everything – the cost of the data, the print, the photography, etc.	
Cost per Item	Cost divided by Distributed	Compare with other activity – and the impact it creates. Is it worth it?
Orders	The number of orders placed as a result of the activity. Possibly tracked by a code the customer gives you, or via the Matchback process	
Value	The value of the orders	Partly depends on what you are promoting. But for cold activity, it will generally be below normal AOVs.
AOV	The average order value. Sales divided by Orders.	
Response Rate	A Percentage. Orders divided by Distributed	Compare with other activity – what do you need to be getting?
Cost/Profit per Order	(Sales minus Cost) divided by Orders	This enables you to compare all the offline activity (and online activity) you are doing – what do you need it to be?
Impressions	How many eyeballs did your advertising get in front of?	
Cost per 1,000 Impressions	Cost divided by Impressions	Enables you to compare the relative costs of different advertising
Brand Recall	Gathered through surveys of the target market. It will show how effectively the advertising has made people more aware of your brand.	
Sign-ups	If there's a Call to Action in the advertising – how many people did it? It might be to sign up for emails, follow on Facebook, or take advantage of an offer.	
Response Rate	A percentage. Sign-ups divided by impressions	Again, you'll learn what works for your business

It is likely that most of the marketing activity you do offline (exclude mailing your housefile) will be unprofitable. So you also need to track how the customers you recruit via each method go on to behave over the coming months: do they keep ordering from you? (For more information on this see the Tip Box about Customer Lifetime Value in Step 3.)

Successful Offline Marketing Checklist

- Can you use offline marketing to improve the response of your housefile?
- Be clear on *why* you are doing offline marketing: branding or sales?
- Prepare for a long testing process.
- Test more than one method.

NOTES

What are the key points from this section?

Other Notes:

WEBSITE
Visit **eCommerceMasterPlan.com**
for more information on Offline Marketing.

Top Tip: MatchBacks: How to properly analyse how offline Direct Mail performs

Back in Part 3, I wrote about the Attribution Debate in online marketing. Well, the Matchback process I'm going to outline here is a way to make sure all the sales from your direct marketing activity are attributed back to the source of the data. This isn't full attribution, as it doesn't go so far as to decide what level of impact each marketing method had on bringing in the sale, nor does it take into account overlaps with online marketing.

The Matchback process is a fairly simple one, but it is essential to use in order to understand how well each of your cold data lists have performed.

When you prepare data for a mailing, you have to de-dupe it to ensure that each person only gets one copy of the mailing. That de-dupe process is necessary because when you are buying and swapping cold lists you will get names of people that are already on your own database, and some people will appear on more than one of the lists you buy. De-duping is a great process for making sure you only mail the right people; but it also means that you are not getting a full picture of how well each list really works for you.

It is also increasingly difficult to track the sales response from Direct Mail because that requires getting the customers to enter a code on the website, or tell you that code when they call up. However good your systems are, you won't capture every response this way.

The Matchback process is designed to counter both these problems.

You run a Matchback at the end of the season to understand how your cold lists really performed, as it will match the sales back to the people on each list. To prepare for a Matchback you need to pull together:

- Each of your original (pre de-dupe) cold mailing files.
- Which lists were sent to who for each mailing.
- How long each mailing was valid for – how long after it mailed you believe it will have generated a response (this is usually between 4 and 8 weeks).
- A full list of orders placed during the season – name, address, and value.

Then you simply reallocate any order that came in from someone on each list during the length that mailing was valid.

This will give you the true value of each data source. The total will be higher than your sales total for the season because you are double counting – but you will get the right metrics to be able to truly compare list performance.

Top Tip: Direct Mail Pointers

Here are a few things it's worth knowing about direct mail and catalogues before you start:

- Printing costs are ruled by the four times table. The better the number of pages in the catalogue fits into the 4 times table, the cheaper it will be to print (per page). So if you can divide it by 16 that's going to be better than if you can only divide it by 8. Therefore a 64-page book is much better than a 56-page one.
- Print your cover separately and use a heavier paper for the cover than the contents. So, your 64-page book becomes a 64-page book with a 4-page cover.
- With a heavy cover, you can get away with a much lighter inner paper – the heavier the paper you use, the more clay is in it, and the more expensive it is.
- Whether you're doing a catalogue or a postcard, try and make the dimensions fit standard dimensions; the size of the mailing piece may well impact on the price of postage, printing, paper, binding, and mailing.
- Consider going naked. If you mail your catalogue without any polywrap, it will save you money, and you can get some environmental discounts, too. Some companies have also reported that it increases response.
- You can rent space in your mailings. If you are sending out a mailing in an envelope or polywrap, you can allow other businesses to insert a leaflet and they'll pay you for the privilege. List brokers are a good place to start if you are interested in doing this. They'll also help you find people who will pay to be included in your product parcels.

Top Tip: Swap vs. Rent Lists

One of the most effective ways to find good cold data is to buy it direct from another eCommerce business. Find a business with similar customers to yours and see if they rent their data.

What's even better is if these companies are interested in your data. Then, you can do a swap: so they allow you to mail 10,000 of their customers and, rather than paying them, you allow them to mail 10,000 of theirs.

Data swaps usually start at 10,000 records or above, and are almost always focused only on data that's bought from you in the last 12 months. So you need to have had 10,000 people buy from you in the last 12 months who are happy for you to sell their data.

You may have to grow further before you can start swapping, but keep it in mind, as once you are able it can make further growth much cheaper.

If you are scared that you may lose customers to the other company – well yes, you might. But you may lose them anyway, and they may lose customers to you. I know a lot of business owners who have shied away from swaps for exactly that reason; almost all of them are now engaged in swapping data, and wish they had done it years ago.

Search Marketing

Search marketing is essential for these eCommerce Business Structures:

- Online Only
- Mail Order
- Big Bricks and Clicks
- Boutique Bricks and Clicks
- Full Multichannel

It is also going to be really powerful for you if your USP is:

- Knowledge and Information – because at the core of any successful search marketing strategy is great content

Why should you use Search Marketing if you are an eCommerce Business?

Search marketing is a source of free traffic to your website. If you can build that traffic up, and make sure it's traffic worth having (traffic that converts to sales), then it can be one of the most effective ways to grow your eCommerce business. It's powerful because:

- If you build your traffic in the right way, you will create a dependable source of traffic, sales, and customers that you don't need to spend much money to attract.

This can be so powerful that for some businesses it can be their USP.

Search Marketing Objectives for eCommerce Businesses

It will take a few months for your Search Marketing activity to pay off; possibly more than a year. So you need to be committed to it for the long haul.
The end objectives (whether that happens within 3 months, 6 months, or 2 years) need to be driving sales and attracting new customers, as well as keeping existing customers coming back to your website to buy.

As it takes a while to pay off, it doesn't mean you don't have to bother tracking its performance. What you need to do is pay close attention to the story that sits under the sales and ROI – so looking at the traffic volumes, the sources of that traffic, how many keywords that traffic comes in via, and also how the traffic behaves on your website. So is it good or bad traffic?

How Search Marketing Works

Search marketing is traffic you get from the search engines that you haven't had to pay for.

By "pay for", I mean that you haven't directly paid for that traffic (like you would with a PPC account). Of course, search marketing isn't free: you may have paid an agency or your website builders, and there's all the time you have spent working on optimising the content and creating it, too.

The search marketing we are discussing here is broader than just SEO (Search Engine Optimisation). SEO is focused on getting you to position Number One by optimising your website and getting inbound links. Search marketing is now far more complex than just SEO because:

- **Universal Search** means that there are now multiple ways to get into the search results – there are the map results, the product search results, social media results, image results, video, and more.
- **Increasingly Sophisticated Algorithms** mean that trying to manipulate the 'normal' search results (the preserve of SEO) is becoming dangerous – in 2012 you are likely to be penalised for activity that was considered 'good' in 2011.

It is possible to spend many hours and days trying to work out what the latest changes mean, and how to 'do SEO' in order to keep your traffic volumes up; but that's time that could be better spent elsewhere. I prefer to keep in mind where Google is actually trying to get to.

A few years ago Larry Page (co-founder and CEO of Google) described the "perfect search engine" as something that:

"…understands exactly what you mean and gives you back exactly what you want".

So Google are trying to provide each individual person with their perfect results. That gives us the third reason we are talking about Search Marketing and not just SEO here:

- **Personalised Search** is here. Google gives you different results based on where you are in the world (just search for takeaway); if you are logged into Google it will also give you results based on websites you have been to before; and if you have a Google+ account, the results you see will be influenced by what people you are connected to have looked at and Liked. This is just the tip of the iceberg.

The pace of change in the search engine world is increasing.

How Do we Manage the Changes? What Do we Need to Do?

At the highest level, we need to try and make sure our website is the best possible result for our keywords, so the site is frequently "exactly what you want".

Practically, this means:

- Take advantage of every route into the search results as possible
- Create great content that customers will appreciate
- Optimise your website with the right keywords

I am going to run through what you need to do in each of these below.

Take advantage of every route into the search results as possible

New routes in are appearing fairly frequently, so you need to keep an eye on what is appearing in the actual search results for your products and keywords. Then you can take advantage of new routes quickly.

Currently, the key routes in are as follows, and all of these are essentially free:

Route In	What and how
Google Base aka Product Search aka Google Merchant Centre Tool: HYPERLINK "http://www.google.com/merchants" www.google.com/merchants Results: HYPERLINK "http://www.google.co.uk/shopping" www.google.co.uk/shopping	**What** Essential for any eCommerce business, Google Merchant Center is how you get your products to appear in the Shopping Results section of Google. This is frequently appearing in the normal results now – especially at a key product level. It's a great place to be, because your products are appearing in front of people who are looking for just that product – so great conversion, and frequently new customers. **How** First you need to create a Google Merchant account, then create a feed and submit the feed into Google via your Merchant account. There are key things that Google needs to see in your feed, so follow the instructions carefully. In your feed, you will need a link back to the product page and to the image for the product on your server; it's generally best to have the feed created from your website. You can also usually get this set up so it automatically updates and feeds into Google every 24 hours or so.
Image Search Results: HYPERLINK "http://www.google.co.uk/imghp" www.google.co.uk/imghp	**What** This is Google's search engine of images. If you sell products that are particularly decorative, then this can be really powerful. **How** Google automatically picks up images from your website. So you can't exactly feed them straight into Google. But you can optimise your images. That means getting all the text around them right – the alt text, the anchor text (if they link somewhere), and the content on the page the image sits on. You can also add image information to the sitemap XML feed you provide via webmaster tools.

Route In	What and how
Google Maps aka Google Place Pages aka Google+ Place Pages Tool: HYPERLINK "http://www.google.com/local/add/businessCenter" www.google.com/local/add/businessCenter or via Google+ Results: maps.google.co.uk	**What** These are the results that appear on Google Maps, and also in the search results as locations. So if you have physical locations that people can visit, it's well worth getting your Place Page created and optimised. **How** The first thing to do is find out if you already have a place page. Google have created many automatically, if your business is already on Google Maps then you need to take control and confirm you are the business owner – a set of fairly simple steps. If your business isn't already there, you simply need to go to Google's Local Business pages register and get it set up. Once it's there, you can encourage people to review your business and also update it with any events or promotions you are running.
Video Results Tool: HYPERLINK "http://www.YouTube.com/" www.YouTube.com Results: HYPERLINK "http://www.google.com/videohp" www.google.com/videohp	**What** These are results that are videos. **How** You don't have to have your video on YouTube to appear here (but as YouTube is the second biggest search engine worldwide it would make sense to have it there, too; it also makes hosting really easy), but it helps. If you want your videos to only be on your website, then you need to provide a Video XML to Google via Webmaster Tools. Plus make sure you have optimised your video, too.
News Tool: support.google.com/news/publisher Results: news.google.com	**What** The news results are a Google manipulation of world news. When a story is a hot topic, the news results will show on the normal search results – often at the top. **How** If your site is a news source in its own right then you can submit it for inclusion in Google News. You can also create a news sitemap and submit that via Webmaster Tools. If you only have an occasional story to submit, you can't do that directly. So you will need to get it onto a site that is being included in Google News. Several of the PR newswires fit into this category.

Once you have got into the results, all of these can be optimised.

> **WEBSITE**
> More details on the current options and methods are on ecommerceMasterPlan.com/free

Create great content that customers will appreciate

As well as getting yourself noticed by the Google radar in as many ways as possible, what can you do to make sure you are going to get seen and therefore get the traffic you deserve?

You have got to have the right content – and it's got to be great content. Clearly, if you don't have videos or news content, you are already out of the running in two of the routes in; so you need to start creating some.

It also needs to be content people want to read and want to share: that's the definition of great. It's even greater if it is content your target customers want to read and share.

So as well as creating the content on your website, you also need to make sure you have got your Social Sharing buttons in place (see page 118 Social Media for more on that). Google is possibly now seeing social shares as more important than inbound links – not least because they are harder to fake – so you need to be doing everything you can to encourage your customers to share your content and talk about you on social media.

For more information on how to create content see Section 2.

Optimise your website with the right keywords

> **WORKBOOK**
> Download our Search Keywords Workbook from the website at ecommerceMasterPlan.com/Free

Every piece of content you create needs to be optimised. The product pages on the website, your blog posts, your videos, your images. How you do this for each type of content does vary a bit; but in each case it is really critical to get the keywords right.

So far we have discussed how to get into the search engine results (the table of routes), and how to make Google think you are important enough to be seen on the first page (content and social media), but we've not looked at how to make sure you appear for the correct things.

Optimising your search traffic is all about making sure you are getting traffic that is interested in buying your products rather than just traffic. Optimising that traffic is mainly about what keywords you go after. Getting the keywords in your content and on your website correct can be really powerful. I frequently see getting this right for people have a massive impact on their traffic, and more importantly creating conversions – sometimes even doubling them!

Getting the keywords on your website right has the quickest impact of any search marketing activity, because it makes a difference to how Google sees your website almost overnight. Getting the keywords right is in two key stages: first you identify the right keywords, then you need to get them onto the website:

– Identify the right keywords

Finding the right keywords isn't difficult – but it's important to do it right.

First you need to brainstorm what the keywords for your website might be. Don't just do this yourself – ask the rest of the business. Once you have got all those suggestions, gather them in an Excel spreadsheet. Then look at what keywords have brought you traffic in the past (you should be able to get this from Google Analytics): add that to the spreadsheet. If you have PPC on the go (or ever have), get the keywords from that as well, and add them to the spreadsheet.

At this point you may also want to consult a few keyword tools (the Google one is pretty good, and free) to see what keywords you have missed. Add these to the spreadsheet.

Once you have your very large spreadsheet, you need to gather some data on those keywords so you can see what is good and what is bad. So add the following data in for each keyword:

- Traffic volumes – you can get this from many tools; you can get it from Google Keyword Tool for free.
- Google Analytics Data – what the keywords have previously done for you. At a minimum, you want Visits, Conversions, and Bounce Rate.
- PPC Data – again, to see what the keywords have previously done for you. At a minimum you want Visits and Conversions.
- Where your website is right now on the search engines – so a ranking report on all the keywords, too.

It will take a while to gather the data and even longer to analyse it, but it's worth it. Once you have considered all the data you should be able to see:

- Which keywords offer the biggest opportunity – those with large traffic volumes
- Which keywords work for you – those that have converted in the past and have low bounce rates
- Which keywords you are going to win on the fastest – those you are already ranking well for, or already getting traffic from

Now you have found the best keywords to aim for, you need to get them onto your website.

– Get the keywords onto your website

The first step is to tie the keywords to pages: which page would be the best for each keyword to be on? You want a page that is about the keyword (you don't want to put "curtains" on a page about wall paint), and you want it as close to the homepage as possible – so either the homepage or a category page. You might find that the results of the keyword analysis lead you to want to change some of the site's structure and create new pages where the search opportunities are. Bear in mind you only really want one or two keywords per page.

Once that is done, you'll probably have between 5 and 20 pages keywords that you want to optimise. We are going to get the rest of the site optimised automatically; that's one of the great things you can do really easily with an eCommerce website.

To get the keywords onto the pages, we need to get them in the right places:

- Title Tag – the most important place for your keywords (consumers don't really see this).
- Meta Description Tag – not critical, but you do need it to be different on every page, so it is worth doing at the same time (consumers don't really see this).
- H tags – these are the headings in the copy on the page, and are usually your Category and product names. You want just one H1 tag, and then more H2s and H3s.
- For images, you also want to get the alt text right.

Your H tag changes are best done by improving the category and product names. So we are going to focus on the other three here.

For your chosen pages you will need to write the Title Tag and Meta Description tag. The Title tag should be relatively short and have the keywords at the beginning (apart from the homepage, where the first words need to be your brand name). The meta-description needs to be about the page, for example:

Title tag: Ladies Red Shoes from the shoe shop
Meta Description: At the shoe shop we stock a wide range of ladies shoes in red, including boots, slingbacks, court shoes, and sandals. Order today for free delivery in the UK.

Once they are all written, you need to put them in place on the website. You might be able to do this via your CMS, but if not, your website builder will be able to do it for you.

Then you need to get the automatic tags done. For this you will almost certainly need to brief your website builder. You'll need to provide them with a brief covering the following:

- The automatic tagging on the pages should also work for new pages that are created. This should be a one-off exercise.
- If a tag is supplied manually, that should overwrite the automatic tagging.
- Alt text on all product images should be set as: "[product name] from the shoe shop"
- Title tag on all product pages should be set as "[product name] – [category name] from the shoe shop"
- Title tag on all category pages should be set as "[category name] from the shoe shop"
- Title tag on all other pages should be set as "[page name] from the shoe shop"
- Meta-description on all product pages should be set as "At the shoe shop we stock a wide range of [product name], including boots, slingbacks, court shoes, and sandals. Order today for free delivery in the UK".
- Meta-description on all category pages should be set as "At the shoe shop we stock a wide range of [product name], including boots, slingbacks, court shoes, and sandals. Order today for free delivery in the UK".
- Meta-description on all other pages should be set as "[page name]. At the shoe shop we stock a wide range of [product name], including boots, slingbacks, court shoes, and sandals. Order today for free delivery in the UK".

As soon as Google picks up on all of that being in place (usually within a week), you should see an immediate impact in search traffic to your website and more keywords driving that traffic.

Once all this is done, don't think you can forget about your keywords. You need to review whether or not you chose the right ones. Did they bring in conversions? If not you may need to amend them in 6 or 12 months' time. You also need to keep remembering what you most important keywords are as you create and optimise your content, and keep focusing on them.

When Doesn't Search Marketing work?

If you have a site built-in flash it's going to be harder to optimise it to get your traffic from search. Other than that, every business selling online should be aware of how to get traffic from the search engines. Even if you are using someone else's website, getting the keywords for your products right will bring you more sales.

What to Measure in Search Marketing

MARKETING PERFORMANCE REPORT

Traffic Source	Visits	Bounce Rate	Cost	Orders	Value	AOV	Conversion Rate	Sales/Visit
Google	5,000	30.00%	2,000	26	1,820	70	5.00%	36.4p
Base	5,000	35.00%	5,00	35	1,575	45	8.00%	31.5p

From this, you can see that Google Analytics is going to be your Number One tool.

Below are the key metrics you need to be measuring for your search marketing; most are in the table above. The performance of your search marketing will improve over time, so don't worry if on day one some of your statistics are way off the benchmarks. The best way to measure it is to compare the trends over time:

SEARCH MARKETING METRICS

Metric	What is it?	Benchmarks
Visits	How much traffic got to your website from each Search traffic source (Base, Places, Google, AOL, etc.)	
Bounce Rate	A percentage A bounce is someone who gets to your website, looks at one page, and then leaves – it's a good indicator of how good quality your traffic is	A good Bounce Rate is below what your website achieves overall If you are getting a good conversion rate from the Search traffic then you can worry less about the bounce rates

Metric	What is it?	Benchmarks
Orders	The number of orders placed as a result of each search marketing channel Tracked via Google Analytics	
Conversion Rate	A percentage Orders divided by Clicks	This should be in line with your website's average Conversion Rate
Sales	The value of the orders	
AOV	The average order value Sales divided by Orders	This partly depends on what traffic you are driving to the website, e.g. traffic from Base may convert at a low AOV as they only buy one item. But generally it should be in line with normal AOVs.
Sales per Visit	A great way to compare the performance of traffic sources where visitor volume varies Sales divided by visits	Look at how your website performs overall – that will give you the benchmark you will want your search traffic to be better than
No. of X driving the traffic	For traffic from search engines, this would be the number of keywords, for Base it would be the number of products, for Images, number of images This gives you a view on the visibility you are getting in the search results	Basically, you just want to keep seeing this number getting higher
Impressions	If you have Webmaster Tools integrated with Google Analytics you can get the impressions count	
CTR	You can see your click-through rate This shows how well you have optimised your content	

For the eCommerce business, it should be all about the traffic and how well it converts, not about whether or not you are in first position. Saying that, improving your rankings will increase traffic so it can be useful to check them every three to six months. When you do, as well as running the report also have a look at what the search results page actually looks like; what is being shown there, and how can you get into it?

Search Marketing | 155

Successful Search Marketing Checklist

- Have you covered all the routes into the search results that you can?
- Is the website fully optimised? Keywords and tags?
- Have you incorporated Search objectives into your social media activity?
- Are you creating content?

NOTES

What are the key points from this section?

Other Notes:

WEBSITE
Visit **eCommerceMasterPlan.com** for the latest information on Search Marketing, what's new, what Google has done now, and how it all relates to eCommerce businesses.

Top Tip: What are Search Algorithms?

The algorithm is a very complex piece of software that analyses millions of pieces of data to return a result. In search terms, it's the thing that analyses all of the world wide web to work out what appears in the search results you see on Google, or Bing, or another. Each search engine has its own algorithm, and each one assesses the possible results differently. It is how they assess the possible results that is what concerns search marketers; so when you hear about an algorithm change it means that the search engine has changed the way in which it assesses the data, for example:

- Something that previously was important isn't any more (or vice versa)
- They have started taking something into account that they didn't before (or vice versa)
- Or 100 other options

It's very hard to anticipate what the next change will be, and (of course) no search engine tells us exactly what their algorithm does. This is why it's important to focus on what the search engine is trying to achieve rather than the individual changes.

Top Tip: Why Google?

Most search marketers focus on Google because it is the biggest: it has over 80% of the search market in the UK and in the USA. Doing well on Google will bring the most traffic and therefore the most sales.

Google is also the most sophisticated search engine, and the others are playing catch up, so Google's writing the rule book. That means anything you do to be better on Google will probably be the same thing you need to do to be better on the other search engines.

In some countries this isn't the case, as they have a local search engine which is the biggest. In China, the biggest is www.baidu.com, with about 75% of the market share; in Russia, it's HYPERLINK "http://www.yandex.com/" www.yandex.com, with about 60% of the market share. So if you are looking at international sales, make sure you are focused on the right search engine for that marketplace.

Top Tip: DMOZ

DMOZ.org is the Open Directory Project. It is a project to try and human review all websites on the internet. It's important in search marketing because it's highly respected by Google, and is where they send their spiders out from; the spiders research the internet to create Google's index. If you are not on Google's Index you won't get into the search results – so if the spiders don't find you, you won't be on Google.

Luckily DMOZ isn't the only way for Google to find your website, as it frequently takes months (if not years) for someone to review your website, and until you have been reviewed you can't be listed. But it does only take about five minutes to request listing – so make sure you do that for your website.

Top Tip: Webmaster Tools and Sitemaps

Each search engines has a "Webmaster Tools": its site owners' way of talking to the search engine about their performance and what they are doing right or wrong.

It's also a way for website owners to raise their profile with the search engines, because you can submit data to them (via a sitemap) though the tools. Also, you can get extra data about how well your website is doing, and then you can get it fixed!

Finally, on Google, you can integrate your Webmaster Tools and Google Analytics, which gives you some great data about how well you are doing on Google. You can see the number of impressions you have had on each keyword, and also which of your content is appearing the most often – this is really useful data.

To get set up, go to:

For Google: HYPERLINK "http://www.google.com/webmasters/tools/" www.google.com/webmasters/tools/

For Bing: HYPERLINK "http://www.bing.com/toolbox/webmaster/" www.bing.com/toolbox/webmaster/

Don't forget to create your sitemaps and submit them, too.

PPC (Pay Per Click) Marketing

Pay Per Click marketing is essential for these eCommerce Business Structures:

- Online Only

But it can be a highly effective sales driver in many product sectors for all eCommerce Business Structures.

It is also particularly useful if your USP is

- Products or price
- And will work more effectively if your brand is strong

Why should you use PPC if you are an eCommerce Business?

PPC means Pay Per Click. It can be used to refer to any advertising where you pay for each click to your website. For the purposes of this section, we are focusing mainly on search PPC (using either Google Adwords or Microsoft Adcenter), but we will also discuss using it on Facebook and LinkedIn.

PPC marketing can be a really effective way to quickly build a stream of quality traffic to your website. But it will only work well if your products are right for PPC, if there isn't too much competition, and if your offering is good. The strengths of PPC are:

- You get traffic really fast – you don't need to wait for the SEO activity to kick in or until you have a big enough email database. So long as you can afford the clicks you can get traffic to your site within minutes.
- You are in total control – you select where/to whom your ads will be shown, you set how much you are willing to pay, and you can stop it at any time.
- It is very flexible – changing things is very easy, and the changes happen almost immediately, so you can react to changing situations fast. If the product goes out of stock you can stop advertising it immediately.

PPC Marketing Objectives for eCommerce Businesses

PPC activity will mainly be focused on recruiting new customers and on driving sales. It can be expensive, so you don't want to be relying on it to get your existing customers back to you.

How PPC marketing works:

You set up an account with one of the PPC services, create ads, and tell the system how you want those ads targeted (at people searching on a keyword, or those interested in certain things). The ads are then shown, and each time someone clicks on the ad (on a link to a page on your website) then you are charged the agreed fee.

PPC Accounts are VERY easy to set up (under 30 minutes, usually), but take a lot of work to get right. Anyone can use them to generate traffic to their website, but as an eCommerce business you don't just want any old traffic; you want quality traffic – traffic that's going to buy from you. You also need that traffic to not cost you too much. The performance needs to fit with your ROI (profit) objectives.

The good news is that it's very possible to optimise your PPC account to make sure the traffic you get is quality traffic, and to keep it within your ROI objectives. We are going to look at how to optimise later in the section, but before we get into how to do PPC we first need to explain and work out the key number in Pay Per Click.

> **WORKBOOK**
> To make the most of this Section, go to **ecommerceMasterPlan.com/Free** and download the accompanying workbook.

Your Cost/Sales, or "Cost as a percentage of sales"

You'll remember this from Step 3, the Second Core Foundation:

MARGIN AND CONTRIBUTION

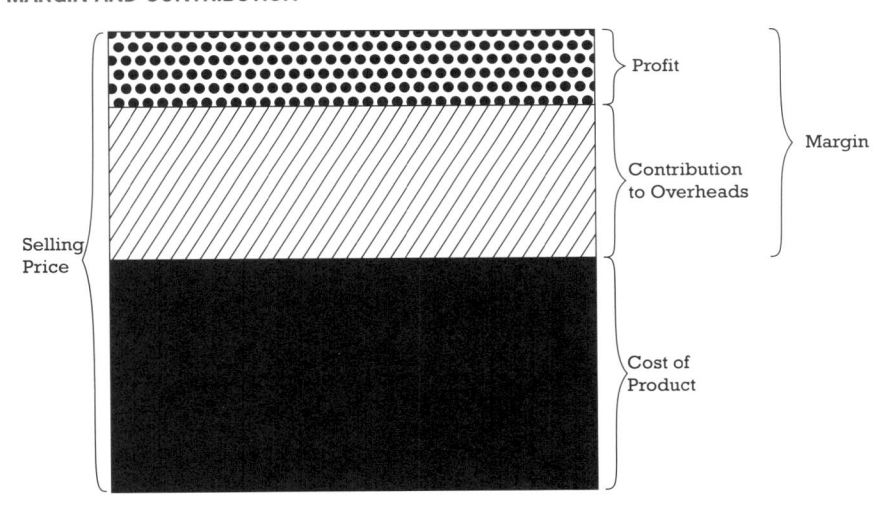

[Diagram showing Selling Price split into: Profit + Contribution to Overheads (together forming Margin) + Cost of Product]

We know that the value of each sale the website generates is split three ways: it covers the cost of the products bought and a contribution to company overheads, and what is left is profit. Part of this profit piece is what you'll be spending on click costs.

It might also be that to gain a new customer you are happy to lose money. Whether that's the case or not, if you know the numbers above, it's easy to work out what percentage of each sale you are willing to spend on click costs: that is your Cost/Sales.

This is a really useful number to have because it makes it REALLY EASY to see how well your PPC activity is doing. Almost every PPC report you'll ever look at has the cost and the sales figure – so it gives you all the numbers you need to see if you are on target or not.

Most businesses will need to run at Cost/Sales of 20% or higher to get enough traffic for the activity to be worthwhile.

PPC Structure and Strategy

The Number One key to successful PPC is to get your account set up correctly. The following is based on Google Adwords structure, but Microsoft Adcenter works in a very similar way.

The basic structure is:

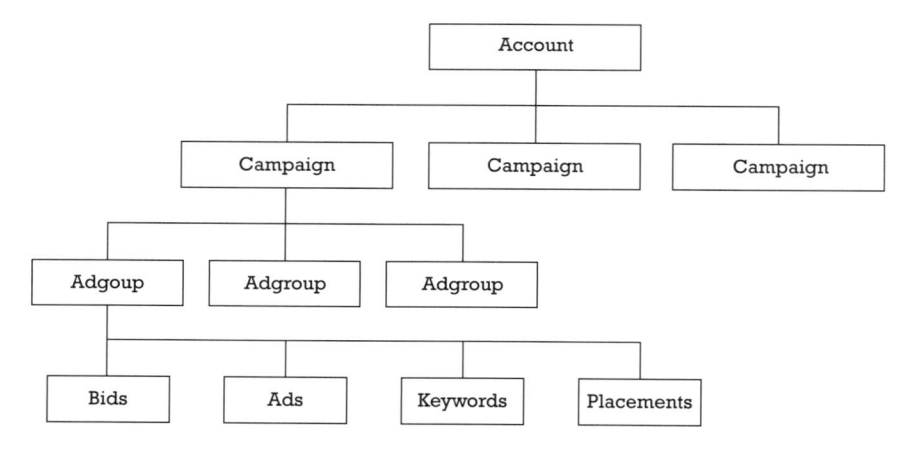

```
                        Account
          ┌───────────────┼───────────────┐
       Campaign        Campaign        Campaign
   ┌──────┼──────┐
Adgoup  Adgroup  Adgroup
   ┌──────┬──────┬──────┐
  Bids   Ads  Keywords Placements
```

Before you start building your account, you need to carefully consider how it's going to be structured. There are two things to take into account:

1. **Reporting**
   It is really easy to produce reports at Campaign Level and Adgroup Level. So you should structure these to be areas you might want to look at.
2. **Optimisation and Quality Score**
   The game with PPC is to get the best traffic possible for the lowest possible cost. That means taking everything to the nth degree and really focusing on the niches. But practicality comes into play, so we're not going to go as far as to create one adgroup for each individual product straight away; but that is where we might end up. We need each adgroup to be full of very similar keywords that can all use the same ads and link to the same landing page.
   This also makes the account much easier to use and to optimise.

So how should you structure your account? For an eCommerce business, this should be relatively straightforward, because the structure of your PPC account should broadly follow the structure of your website – so long as that's well structured! We are going to run through an example for a clothing retailer here, which will help to make everything a lot clearer for you.

– Example Fashion Retailer Campaigns
- Brand
- Women
- Men's
- Children

The campaigns are split out this way so we can see at a glance how the different genders are performing, and work out how to allocate the budget between them (you can only set daily budget limits at Campaign level).

– Example Fashion Retailer Adgroups in the Womenswear Campaign

- Mini-skirts
- Maxi-skirts
- A-Line skirts
- Knee-length skirts
- Trousers
- Jeans
- Shirts
- Blouses
- Sandals
- Boots
- Shoes
- Belts
- Jackets
- Coats
- Casual Dresses

The adgroups are split out by product type: you can easily see above how the keywords in each adgroup are going to be focused. We have several adgroups for skirts because the types of skirt are very different. The blouse and shirt adgroups will both go to the same landing page, but some women call them shirts and some blouses, so we're going to cover both with the keywords and they will perform better is the adtext matches the keywords. For the dresses, we only have a "causal" option because "Dresses" is an extremely competitive keyword, so we can't afford to be non-specific.

Now we have the structure for Womenswear, it will be pretty easy to roll out to Children and Men's.

Brand Bidding

One of the oldest questions in PPC is: should you bid on your own name? The short answer is yes, because:

- As we saw on page 146, the search engine results are constantly changing, so we need to create as many ways as possible to be there, and PPC is one.
- Being in first position and having the paid ad gives you much more of the available real estate, thus increasing the chances of being clicked on.
- Some people click paid ads, some click non-paid.
- It's really not very expensive – you should be paying a lot less than 10p per click, and the ROI should be huge. So it's a fairly cheap insurance policy to make sure your customers find your website.

You may also have noticed that there's a separate "Brand" campaign in the example above. That is because if you are going to bid on brand keywords, you want to measure their performance separately from the rest of your activity. Their performance will be phenomenal, and you don't want to think the rest of your PPC is doing better than it really is because you have grouped it with your brand activity.

In your Brand adgroup, you should include your brand name, your website address, and common misspellings: phonetic and typos. So for indiumonline (my marketing agency), we bid on keywords such as these: indium, indyum, iridium, indian.

How to Optimise

The key to successful PPC is to optimise.

From the day you first launch your PPC activity, you will never stop needing to optimise it. It will also take several months to get it performing properly, when you first start it all.

We have already worked out our target for performance – the Cost/Sales percentage. So what we need to do to optimise the account is:

- Identify the activity that is failing to meet that target and penalise it. Either turn it off, or optimise it down.
- Identify the activity that is performing ahead of that target and optimise it up.

We can analyse at lots of levels: Campaign, Adgroup, Keyword, and Placement, so it's important to fully understand what is happening before optimising badly.

For example:

Target Cost/Sales = 30%

Our Women's Campaign is performing at 40%

Should we turn it off? Let's look deeper:

Within the Women's Campaign, all adgroups are within the target, apart from "Jeans", which is at 60%

Should we turn it off? No, let's look deeper:

Within Jeans adgroup, we have 10 keywords; 5 of those are performing within the target, 4 have yet to drive a sale, and the keyword "Jeans" is performing at 70%

By looking deeper, we have identified that the only issue is the keyword "Jeans", so we need to optimise it down.

OPTIMISING UP AND DOWN

Level	Optimise Up	Optimise Down
Keyword	Increase bid Add more keyword match types	Decrease bid Change match type to a more strict one Pause
Adtext	Create another copy Pause other ads	Turn off Test a different version Try linking to a different page
Placements	Turn into a managed placement Increase the bid	Decrease the bid Turn it into a negative placement (so your ads don't appear there)
Adgroups	Increase default bid Split out into more niche adgroups	Decrease default bid Pause
Campaigns	Increase budget Widen targeting	Decrease budget Pause

These are the key ways to optimise your account. There are others and they change over time as Microsoft and Google create new tools, but these are your key methods.

Before you get cracking with your optimisation, what we also need to understand is how much we need to spend on each keyword before we know if it works or doesn't. This is your AOV multiplied by your Cost/Sales percentage.

For example:

Cost/Sales Percentage = 30%
AOV = £50

The amount you need to spend before you can validly give up on a keyword = £15

If the AOV was £100, it becomes £30

It is important to understand this number so you know when to turn off a keyword. If you start turning off keywords that have only had £5 spent on them then you are a long way from knowing if that keyword would work for you or not.

Ads and Landing Pages

With an eCommerce site, you are often restricted in how much you can do with your landing pages. After all, if you are bidding on "Trousers" you want to link to the trousers category – there's not much choice beyond that. But where you do have options it's always good to test them; see which traffic converts best on each page.

Your landing page is a facet of your ad, and there is so much you can test within the ads, and that you should be testing. Generally I recommend people to get the keyword optimisation right before starting on the adtext testing, and the table below show the first things you want to start testing with your ads:

ADTEXT TESTING ELEMENTS

Element	What to test	Lessons to roll out?
Headline	Including your brand name or not The text itself Capitalisation	Brand name or not Capitalisation
Body text	Including your brand name or not The text itself Capitalisation Including the price Including delivery price	Including your brand name or not Capitalisation Including the price Including delivery price
Display URL	Including www. or not Capitalisation Domain vs. something afterwards, e.g. yourdomain.com or yourdomain.com/widget	Including www. or not Capitalisation Domain vs. something afterwards, e.g. yourdomain.com or yourdomain.com/widget

Only ever test one of these at a time within an adgroup. When you learn that something is possible to roll out do, but check that performance does improve everywhere.

Placements and the Content Network

Most of what we've discussed so far in this section has been exclusively about using keywords to advertise within the search engine results of Google (via Google Adwords), Yahoo, or Bing (both via Microsoft Adcenter). There is another set of ads open to you if you are using either of these tools, and which you should be testing and optimising. These are the Placements, and they put your adverts onto websites.

Google chooses when to show your adverts based on how well the keywords in your adgroup match the content of a web page. So if your adgroup is about curtains, your ads will start to appear on websites about interior design and curtains. This should be a good thing, but you need to keep an eye on the performance, optimising individual placements up and down depending on their performance.

At the extreme there are some adgroups where you will want to stop using Placements altogether, and you can do this. There will also be some placements that work so well you will want to create an adgroup for them so you can maximize your return from them.

Stay in Control of your Testing

The danger with PPC is that there's so much to test you just go test crazy, and then it becomes very hard to work out what's causing any uplift in results.

To counter this, keep a record of what you are testing (as simple as a work document or notepad) and remember to check it.

The other thing you should do is timetable your roll-outs. We saw above that it takes a while to optimise an account, and that during that time you are going to be spending a lot of click-cost on seeing if things work. So it's much better to test and optimise some of your activity, then, once you have that optimised, turn on some more. This will speed up the optimisation too, so you'll start to see good results sooner, for example:

If you need to drive 1,000 clicks though an adgroup to optimise it, the total cost of those clicks is £500 (at 50p per click), and your budget is only £200 per month, you are going to do much better if you spend months 1 and 2 getting that adgroup right. Then, by month 3, you'll be driving sales pretty effectively. So you can now start the process again by launching the next adgroup. This also means you can factor in what you learnt with the adgroup 1, so it should be quicker and cheaper to optimise adgroup 2.

When Doesn't PPC Work?

I mentioned at the beginning that PPC doesn't work for every business. Why is that?

- In some sectors, the competition levels are so high that the price of a click means that you can't buy the traffic effectively.
- In other sectors, it's hard to find keywords that identify the searchers as your potential customers well enough.
- Other sectors are so price sensitive that you will get a lot of consumers price comparing and not coming back to you to buy.
- Some products (like jewellery) are very style conscious – so it's hard to get the conversion.

The Changing Face of PPC

Microsoft and Google are constantly changing PPC: what you can do, what you can't, and all kinds of settings options. It's really important to keep on top of this, as fundamentally they are making the changes to make sure you keep spending more with them, not to improve your return – so not all the changes are going to suit you.

In this section we have run through the key fundamentals that haven't really changed over the last 5 years, and which remain the core of PPC success.

WEBSITE
On the website **eCommerceMasterPlan.com**, we have content examining the new things that come and go in PPC, and how to make use of them. Please do check in every now and then, or sign up to the newsletter to make sure you are up to date.

On Facebook and LinkedIn

In addition to paying per click advertising on the search engines, you can now also do it on Facebook and LinkedIn. These operate in a very similar way to the search engines, but with one key difference: you are targeting people based on who they are rather than on what they are looking for.

This can be very cool: for example, if you sell wedding favours you can target people whose Facebook relationship status is "Engaged"; if you sell equestrian clothing, you can target people interested in horses. If you sell stair lifts you can target those aged over 70. But it is much harder to make these ads work within your ROI targets than with PPC. So if you want to head in this direction: test and monitor.

What to Measure in PPC Marketing

PPC MARKETING PERFORMANCE REPORT

Campaign	Impressions	Clicks	CTR %	Cost	Cost per Click	Orders	Value	AOV	Conversion Rate	Cost/Sales
A	50,000	1,500	3.00%	555	37p	30	2,100	70	2.00%	26.40%
B	40,000	400	1.00%	180	45p	12	540	45	3.00%	33.30%

Opposite are the key metrics you need to be measuring for your PPC marketing; most are in the table above:

PPC MARKETING METRICS

Metric	What is it?	Benchmarks
Impressions	The number of times your ad has been seen	
Clicks	The number of clicks on your advert	
CTR %	A percentage The click-through rate Clicks divided by Impressions	This will vary depending on the targeting of the activity. In search PPC, expect it to be between 1% and 10%. If you are bidding on your brand name, it will probably be in double figures. If your activity is also on the content network then CTR will be lower. In social media PPC, expect it to be a fraction of a percent.
Cost	How much you paid for that piece of activity	
Cost per Click	Cost divided by Clicks	
Orders	The number of orders placed as a result of the PPC activity. This is tracked either via the tool you are using or Google Analytics	
Sales	The value of the orders	
AOV	The average order value Sales divided by Orders	Will vary wildly depending on what you are promoting. Advertising socks will have a lower AOV than advertising sofas.
Conversion Rate	A percentage Orders divided by Clicks	Like the AOV and CTR, this really depends on what you are advertising, and how strong your product range is.
Cost/Sales	A percentage Cost as a percentage of the Sales Cost divided by Sales	For a brand adgroup this should be very small – under 5%. For the rest, you need to be willing to spend between 20% and 40% of the sales on clicks.

You should use these tables to compare the performance of your PPC activity at any level; so from comparing Google Adwords and Microsoft Adcenter to comparing individual keywords or placements.

If you are running your PPC accounts well, you will be constantly optimising your activity, so it's really important to look at the results over lots of different time periods. I like to look at the last month and the last 3 months simultaneously, and also to compare what's happening now with what happened last year at the same time.

Successful PPC Marketing Checklist

- Know how much you can afford to spend to get each sale (your Cost/ Sales).
- Keep an eye on the settings and be ready for any changes Google makes.
- Create and follow a launch and optimisation calendar.
- Keep an eye on what's happening in the business and make sure the PPC activity reflects this. Turn off products that aren't in stock, create ads for new products.
- Test, test, test.
- Regularly review the results.

NOTES

What are the key points from this section?

Other Notes:

WEBSITE
Visit **eCommerceMasterPlan.com** for the latest information on PPC Marketing, including what's changing and how to make the most of it.

Top Tip: Quality Score

The Quality Score (QS) is used by Microsoft and Google to assess the quality of your adverts. It is a mark, out of ten, given so that you can access at keyword level on each tool.

10 is best, and to get a 10 your keyword and ad and landing page (plus the way you are targeting it all) need to be in harmony.

So if your keyword is "blue widgets", your adtext is about blue widgets, and your landing page is a page all about "blue widgets", then you are going to get a high score.

But if your keyword is "widgets", your adtext is about blue widgets, and your landing page is a page all about "blue widgets", then you are going to get a much poorer quality score.

On Microsoft, it shows how likely your ads are to appear.

On Google, it helps to determine where your ads appear; so a good QS means you will get a high position (and more traffic) for less money.

Improving your Quality Score is really important to get the most out of your budget and the best quality traffic. But it's not the only thing you need to worry about. All the optimisation tactics we are discussing in this section support improving your QS, though, and it is good to track it over time.

Top Tip: PPC Glossary

- Adtext = an advert that is just text
- CPC = cost per click
- CTR = click-through rate
- Impression = number of times your ads are seen
- Placement = a website on which your ad appears
- Quality score (QS) = how good your keyword/ad/landing page is
- Bid = how much you are willing to pay for a click

Top Tip: Keyword Match Types

We have mentioned these in the optimisation section, and you really need to understand these if you are going to be running successful PPC activity.

There are four keyword match types:

THE FOUR KEYWORD MATCH TYPES

Match Type	Example	How it works	Where in the account?
	What it looks like in your account		
Broad	Red dress	You ads will appear for any search where Google or Microsoft feel it will be relevant. That might include: crimson dress dresses in dark pink blue dress	Set up in adgroups
Phrase	"red dress"	You ads will only appear when someone searches on the phrase on its own, or with text before or after the phrase: red dress buy a red dress red dress for Ascot	Set up in adgroups
Exact	[red dress]	Your ads will only display when someone searches on red dress – they won't appear for anything else	Set up in adgroups
Negative	-blue	Your ads won't appear for phrases with this keyword in. Frequently used negatives are "second hand", "how to", etc.	Either at campaign or adgroup level

It is often worthwhile running a keyword that performs as well as all the match types, because you'll get a different response from each.

Remarketing

Remarketing is essential for these eCommerce Business Structures:

- Online Only
- Mail Order
- Big Bricks and Clicks
- Boutique Bricks and Clicks
- Full Multichannel

It is not particularly useful for any individual USP, but if you are in a very competitive marketplace where customers shop around for the best offer or product, remarketing is a must: it will keep your website in the customers' thoughts.

Why should you use Remarketing if you are an eCommerce Business?

Remarketing (also known as Retargeting) will make all your marketing activity more effective – so you'll have more sales and your marketing budget will go further. Essentially it increases the ROI of all your marketing (both on and offline).

Does this sound too good to be true? It's not a magic bullet, and you have to manage it, but used correctly it will bring great rewards. It is powerful because:

- You get the results very quickly - you are advertising to people who have already been to your site and seen the products, so they know what you are about and are already in the buying cycle.
- You are in total control – you are in control of the adverts and how much you are willing to pay for them. You also control who the ads are shown to, which pages of the site they had to view first, and the demographics of those people. So you are well in control of how efficiently the activity works and how strong the ROI becomes.
- You are targeting people you have already driven to your website once – so you are improving the performance of everything else. Most eCommerce websites will convert at less than 10%, meaning that 90% of visitors leave without giving you any information or buying. Remarketing targets those people, aiming to get them back to buy again.
- It should always be profitable – because you are in control of everything, it should always be possible to optimise it to be profitable.

Remarketing Objectives for eCommerce Businesses

Remarketing activity should be focused on getting a good conversion rate, and getting the right ROI. You have already paid to get these customers to your website once, so the remarketing activity MUST hit your profit targets.

HOW REMARKETING WORKS

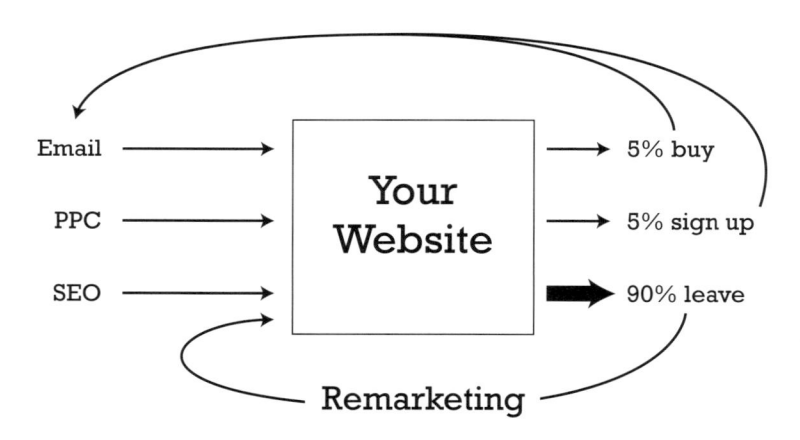

```
Email  ──►  ┌──────────┐  ──►  5% buy
PPC    ──►  │   Your   │  ──►  5% sign up
            │ Website  │
SEO    ──►  │          │  ──►  90% leave
            └──────────┘
                  ▲
                  └──── Remarketing ────┘
```

Remarketing enables you to advertise to people who have already been on your website in order to bring them back to buy from you again. This is done by dropping a cookie on the computer of people who visit certain pages of your site.

So although throughout this section I'm going to be talking about targeting people, as with anything to do with cookies you are actually targeting a certain machine. So if I visit your website on my home laptop and have a remarketing cookie dropped on me, the remarketing ads will also appear when anyone else uses my home laptop, and I won't see the remarketing ads when I use a different computer (unless I have been to your website on that computer, too).

ELEMENTS OF REMARKETING

What you control	Why is it important?
Software	The programme you use to serve the ads
Website tagging	Which pages of the website you capture the visitors of
Cookie lengths	How long you keep visitors in your targeting – how long they see your ads for after they arrive on your site
Ads	Gets the customer to the website
Ad frequency	How many times per day does each person see your ads?
Segmentation	Who sees your ads? (which pages of the site have they been to, what demographics, etc.)

Of these, the software is the only thing you can forget about once it's done; the other five need to be constantly monitored and considered within your optimisation process.

Choosing your Remarketing Platform

For many businesses, the choice of software is very limited: the only viable option is the

> **WORKBOOK**
> Download our helpful Remarketing Workbook that fits with this section at
> **eCommerceMasterPlan.com/Free**

Google Adwords platform.

- Anyone can use the Google remarketing platform – it's just part of the Adwords tool. There are no minimum spend and no set up costs, you can just do it.
- It's always a good idea to test any online marketing before committing to it for the long haul – so the Google platform is the perfect place to do that.
- The other providers essentially have minimum traffic requirements and are only targeting the biggest retailers. Either there is a stated minimum traffic level or the fixed fees are so high you need a certain volume to make it worthwhile.

Although the Google tool is easy to use, it doesn't mean that it's not powerful. The technology is all there, and the ads are shown on the content network – a vast collection of websites set up to display Google Adsense adverts. So your customers will be seeing your ads.

How to start Remarketing

As with any new online marketing tool, it is really tempting to just go and get stuck in. But remarketing is a task where sitting back for a bit and considering your plans can really benefit you.

The Number One rule is to start simply: one ad to everyone.

Although you are using a PPC platform to manage it all, you are targeting and testing people, not keywords. So starting simply and seeing what works is essential.

Website Tagging Structure

The first thing you need to do is get your website tagged; until you have dropped cookies on people you can't start any adverts (because you have got no one to show them to).

Before you brief your website team to put the code in place on the website, there are a few key things to think about. Even though you are going to start off showing the same ad to everyone, you might want to put some future-proofed tagging in place now, so that the website builders are only doing the job once (especially important if you are paying them to do it):

- Before you ads can show, you need to have dropped each cookie on at least 100 people. So each different set of codes you put in place have to drop cookies at least 100 times. Because of this, you want to choose groups of pages that will enable that to happen – so for some websites you might only be able to put one set of code in place, and tag every page.
- To check how quickly you are likely to get 100 people on any set of pages, look at the Page Views count in Google Analytics.
  For which pages do you never want to cookie the people who are looking at them? This might be a complaints page or your email unsubscribe page, if you have one. Simply don't add the code to these pages.
- Do you want to exclude visitors to any page from your remarketing?
  Those who have ordered? Tag these pages with a different code, so you can exclude them.
- Are different product categories likely to bring a different result?
  If you have products with very different AOVs, or some which someone buys quickly whilst another might take more convincing, do you want to treat them differently? Show different ads to them? Or measure how they respond differently?

Remember: you are trying to segment your potential customers based on the pages they view.

After examining all of these possibilities, you will end up with a selection that looks something like this:

EXAMPLE PAGE TAGGING STRUCTURE

Group of pages	Action	Monthly page views
Whole site excluding: - order confirmation - email unsubscribe - print off returns label page	Should be tagged	49,500
Order Confirmation Page	Tag so we can exclude	500
Basket Pages	Tag so we can target those who've added to basket	1,000
Delivery Information Pages	Tag so we can give them an offer on delivery	20
Furniture Categories and Product Pages	Tag to show ads for longer, and see if response is different.	10,000

This should be the activity you are pretty sure you will want to test in the first 6 months. The first selection is your default – this is the one you are going to start with to see how your customers react to remarketing ads. This will give you the benchmark to test everything else against.

The Delivery Information Pages is a great idea. But with only 20 views per month it's not going to work. It will take you 5 months to get enough page views to show ads, and the power of the offer is in how quickly you get it in front of the customer.

Excluding visitors to the Order Confirmation Page is a great move for any eCommerce business; you probably don't want to be trying to get someone who has just ordered back to your website.

The very first activity we are going to do is put remarketing ads in front of the people who have been to the website, but not got to the Order Confirmation page.

If you want to brief all the tagging at once, for everything in the table above, then do. Make sure you keep a record of which sets of codes represent which of your tag ideas. You get the code from Google Adwords when you set up your Remarketing Audience List.

Create a remarketing audience list

The first thing you need to do is create a remarketing audience list. This is in the "Shared Library" (in the left hand menu in Adwords).

A remarketing list is defined by:

- Where you choose to put the code (the tag)
- The duration of the cookie – how many days someone stays in the list after they have most recently been to your website

So give the list a good name and description, and choose the right cookie length. Then you can copy and paste the code you need your website builder to put in place for you.

Build your Remarketing Campaigns

Once the code is in place on the website, you get the adverts and targeting set up.

First, create a new campaign to run this all through, and check all the settings are right (see page 159 on PPC for more detail on this).

Then, create an adgroup for each remarketing campaign you will be running. Your ads will only be showing on the content network – so don't add any keywords.

Navigate into the adgroup, and go into the Display Network tab. Here, you can add your remarketing lists.

Advert Choices

Your remarketing adverts will be appearing on the Content Network – on the Content Network, each website owner chooses what size space they are going to make available for adverts. They also choose what type of ads they are going to allow: image, text, or video, etc.

So to get accurate results and the best chance of success, you want to be using as many of the ad formats as possible.

For your first 'catch everyone list', I strongly advise you to set up a few text ads plus one of every image format as a minimum.

As soon as you have your campaign and your adverts set up, put it live. It might take a few more weeks for there to be enough people to target but you are now ready to take advantage of that, as soon as there will be more than 100.

How to Optimise your Remarketing

Key things to remember when optimising and analysing your remarketing activity:

1. You are optimising people
2. You are not optimising the websites those people are looking at

So do not (until you have done the rest of the optimisation, anyway):

- start using keywords in your remarketing activity
- exclude websites from your remarketing activity (unless they are sites you wouldn't want your brand to appear on)

That leaves you with a few key things you can change to improve performance, and these are the areas you want to focus your optimisation on.

REMARKETING OPTIMISATION

Optimisation option	What/How to test
Adverts – message	What messages work best for you? What offers work well?
Bids	How much are you happy to pay to make sure your ads are appearing?
Tags/Code Structure	How can you better segment your visitors by collecting them into different lists? You may well find yourself creating ads that relate to individual product categories – so you can advertise men's clothes to those who has visited the men's pages.
Demographics	Which age ranges respond best? Are there some you want to exclude from Day 1? (e.g. the under-18s?)
Cookie Lengths	How long after they have been to your site is it still worth showing someone your remarketing ads? (see also Cookie Top Tips)
Geographic	Some areas of the country will buy more from you than others – so this can be useful.
Managed Placements	There may be a handful of sites on the content network that perform better in remarketing for you – those sites that talk about your product, so you know your customer is thinking about the correct things when your ad appears. These will be worth turning into Managed Placements so you can bid higher to make sure you appear more often.
Frequency Capping	This is a general display network setting, set at Campaign level. It restricts how many times your ads are seen by people. You can do that per day, month, week, and at Campaign, adgroup, or even individual ad level.

So although our favourite PPC keywords and placements can't be optimised in Remarketing, there are lots we can optimise.

....

When Doesn't Remarketing Work?

If you can't get the tracking code on the website (because you are PiggyBacking), then you are not going to be able to use Remarketing. But in every other scenario Remarketing should work, as long as your numbers stack up. This is provided you can afford to get people to the website for the first time, and then get them back again via remarketing without it becoming unprofitable. The only way to find that out is to try it, measure it, and optimise it.

What to Measure in Remarketing

REMARKETING PERFORMANCE REPORT

Campaign	Impressions	Clicks	CTR %	Cost	Cost per Click	Orders	Value	AOV	Conversion Rate	Cost/Sales
A	50,000	1,500	3.00%	555	37p	30	2,100	70	2.00%	26.40%
B	40,000	400	1.00%	180	45p	12	540	45	3.00%	33.30%

Below are the key metrics you need to be measuring for your remarketing; most are in the table above, and they are very similar to PPC marketing:

REMARKETING METRICS

Metric	What is it?	Benchmarks
Impressions	The number of times your ad has been seen	
Clicks	The number of clicks on your ad	
CTR %	A percentage The click-through rate Clicks divided by Impressions	This will vary depending on the targeting of the activity. Remarketing activity is on the content network so CTR will be low.
Cost	How much you paid for that piece of activity	
Cost per Click	Cost divided by Clicks	
Orders	The number of orders placed as a result of the remarketing activity Tracked via Google Adwords (or other tool)	Look at both conversions as a result of people clicking on the ads, but also the "View Through Conversions" – these are the people to whom your ads were shown who then bought but didn't click. With remarketing, you'll often find a LOT of these.
Sales	The value of the orders	
AOV	The average order value Sales divided by Orders	Will vary depending on your remarketing. If you are targeting people based on what they were looking at on the website your AOV will reflect that; if it's blanket remarketing then it should be in line with your website's AOV.

Metric	What is it?	Benchmarks
Conversion Rate	A percentage Orders divided by Clicks	The conversion rate should be higher than your average, because these are people who are already part-way through the buying cycle – they are ready to buy.
Cost/Sales	A percentage Cost as a percentage of the Sales Cost divided by Sales	The critical number for remarketing – this needs to be more profitable than your normal activity, because you have already paid for this order once. But of course it will also improve your overall marketing effectiveness, one of the hardest targets to work out.

Use these metrics to compare the performance of your remarketing activity overall, and for any targeted campaigns you have underway.

Successful Remarketing Checklist

- Know how much you can afford to spend to get each sale (your Cost/ Sales)
- Keep an eye on the settings, and be ready for any changes Google makes
- Start broad and then go more targeted
- Test, test, test
- Regularly review the results

NOTES

What are the key points from this section?

Other Notes:

WEBSITE
At the time of writing, Remarketing is still a relatively new tool, so please visit **eCommerceMasterPlan.com** for the latest information on how Remarketing can work for you.

Top Tip: Cookie Lengths

Cookie Lengths are a really important thing to get right because:

- Make them too long and you will be showing your ads to people who last visited your site months ago, so the power of remarketing fades out
- Make them too short and you won't get enough people for your ads to display

In Google remarketing the Cookie length is how long people will stay in that remarketing list after they last visited your website. So if they come again, they go back to Day 1.

When combined with exclusions, the cookie length can be a great way to optimise. Tag the same set of pages with 3 sets of code, each with a different cookie length:

- List A = 15 days
- List B = 30 days
- List C = 45 days

You can then advertise to people based on how recently they have been to your website. For example:

- No offer to   List A
- Free P&P to   List B, excluding List A
                                          (so people who haven't been to the site
                                          for 15 days)
- Free P&P and 10% off to   List C, excluding List B

Top Tip: For when briefing your website team to put your tags in place

- You are likely to want to change the tags fairly often – so it may be worth getting your team to build a tag management system for you.
- It is definitely worth warning your team that you may be making this type of change every 6 months or so, as there may be things they can do behind the scenes to make it easier for them to do it (and thus cheaper for you!).
- How are you going to make sure your tags are always up to date? What happens when new products go onto the website – how does the tagging change at that point? So do you need to add some tags at a template level?
- Give really clear instructions to your team on what pages you do and don't want tagged.

Partnership Marketing

Partnership marketing is essential for these eCommerce Business Structures. It can also be a great marketing tool for all eCommerce Business Structures, particularly:

- Niche PiggyBack
- Full Multichannel

It is also particularly useful if your USPs are:

- Customer Base – in most partnerships, you are trading access to your customer base – so the larger and better that is, the more successful you will be at finding partners.
- Brand – Partnerships are most successful when the two companies involved appeal to the same sort of customers, so a clear brand really helps identify compatible partners.

Why should you use Partnerships if you are an eCommerce Business?

Partnership marketing covers a wide range of options. It is not right for every eCommerce business, but when it works it can be a cheap and reliable way to recruit good quality new customers. It's also a great way to increase brand awareness, too. It's powerful on a number of levels:

- In any Partnership arrangement you are allying your brand with another business's brand – so you can increase the power of your brand if you choose the right partners.
- You can target specific customer groups – by picking the right partners, you will be targeting consumers who are highly likely to be interested in your products.
- It should always be profitable – often Partnerships are "free", so there is a straightforward swap of opportunities. At worst, they are priced in advanced on success – a commission on sales, or a fixed fee per activity. So you are very much in control of costs that should be low.
- They are a great way to target and recruit key new customers and get them buying from you.

Partnership Marketing Objectives for eCommerce Businesses

Partnership activity should be purely focused on recruiting new customers. And it should be a low-cost way to do that.

You also want to make sure you are working with the right partners: those who support and help build your brand.

How Partnership Marketing Works

Put simply, Partnership Marketing is two (or more) businesses agreeing to do some joint marketing, or swap access to their customers. The businesses you partner with don't have to be eCommerce businesses; you might decide to partner with a magazine or blog site.

Usually any costs will be split 50:50, or if it's a partnership for access to a customer base, it will be done for free.

Key Types of Partnerships

Partnership marketing has been around in the mail order world for decades, with companies swapping mailing lists or catalogues to put in each other's parcels. But it has been slow to catch on in the online world – which is surprising considering how much easier and lower risk it is online than offline.

These are the most common methods of Partnership for eCommerce businesses, but they are certainly not the only options – that is only limited by you and your partners' imaginations.

PARTNERSHIP TYPES

Partnership method	How it works
Parcel Bouncebacks	A bounceback is marketing literature put in the parcel that goes to the customer containing what they have bought. You should already be putting your own marketing into your parcels. With a partnership, you agree to swap a defined number of items (usually a catalogue or flyer) with another business. You put theirs in your parcels, and they put your marketing material in their parcels. Don't forget to check how fast they'll get through the marketing materials – you don't want all theirs out within two weeks, and yours taking two months to get out – it needs to be even more than that.
Order confirmation email bouncebacks	Same principle as for the parcel bouncebacks, only this time you include a banner or link to your partner in your order confirmation emails.
Order Confirmation Page Bounceback	This can be really powerful – as soon as someone's bought from you, you show them an advert for your partner. It's particularly good because (i) they have already bought from you today, (ii) they are in a buying mood.
Email Advertising	This is when you each agree to send an email about the other to your database. So you'll send an email to your customers recommending them. That could be a whole email about them, or it might just be a banner about them. Make sure that you are both sending to a similar volume, and also quality, of people – you don't want to be sent to their enquirer list if you are sending them to your best buyers.
Website Advertising	You each put a banner for the other on your websites. Don't forget to agree how long it will be up for, and where.
Social Media Mentions	This could be blog posts, tweets, retweets, Facebook competitions, or more.

WORKBOOK
To help you get your Partnerships set up, we have created a handy Workbook. Download it from the website: **eCommerceMasterPlan.com/Free**

How to Set up a Partnership

There are two key things that make a successful partnership marketing campaign:

1. The two partners have similar brand values, and target the same customers. For example, Screwfix and New Look wouldn't work; but Boden and Waitrose does.
2. There has to be enough in it for both parties, and that might not be the same thing.

If you are interested in getting a Partnership up and running, you need to first work out who you would like to partner with. Which brands do you customers also like? Who do they also shop with? A simple way to find that out is to ask them! Just run a survey to find out where else they shop. (Surveymonkey is a great tool for this.)

Once you have identified which businesses you want to partner with (and I'd aim to have a list of at least ten) you need to get in contact with them. Call them, email them, DM them on Twitter, send them a letter, connect on LinkedIn – it can take a while to get to them, and to the right person.

When you get talking about the options, have a clear idea of what you can offer and what you would like from them in return. They might not be aware of the concept – you may need to convince them it's a good one, and that it won't annoy their customers, so use some examples of other people who are already doing it. If you have previously done it then show them the results.

If everyone's happy, make sure you get everything in writing. You don't necessarily need to go to the lawyers, but make sure there is a document you are all in agreement on. Include it in all the details: time scales, what's being done, volumes, tracking codes, etc.

Then you can get on with the activity. Once done, don't forget to review the results – and see if it's worked well for them, too. If it has, you should be able to get them to agree to continue with it, or try something else.

Partnerships are all about building up a trusting fair relationship with another business in order to create benefits for you both.

When Doesn't Partnership Marketing Work?

In one form or another, partnership marketing can work for any business, of any size, in any marketplace (not just eCommerce). My online marketing agency partners with other marketing agencies to provide their clients with online marketing services. My social media training agency partners with Trade Bodies to provide their members with tailored training. Microsoft partners with computer manufacturers to have its software pre-installed on computers.

Partnerships are everywhere, and if you follow the process above and find the right partners then they will work for you, too.

What to Measure in Partnership Marketing

PARTNERSHIP MARKETING PERFORMANCE REPORT

Partnership Tactic	Visits	Bounce Rate	Orders	Value	AOV	Conversion Rate	Sales/ Visit
X Email	5,000	30.00%	26	1,820	70	5.00%	36.4p
Y Conf Page	5,000	35.00%	35	1,575	45	8.00%	31.5p

Below are the key metrics you need to be measuring for your Partnership marketing; most are in the table above:

PARTNERSHIP MARKETING METRICS

Metric	What is it?	Benchmarks
Visits	The number of visitors getting to your website as a result of that Partnership activity (remember to add Google tracking code to all links)	
Bounce Rate	A percentage A bounce is someone who gets to your website, looks at one page, and then leaves – it's a good indicator of how good quality your traffic is.	A good Bounce Rate is below what your website achieves overall. If you are getting a good conversion rate from the Partnership traffic you can worry less about the bounce rates.
Orders	The number of orders placed as a result of the activity Tracked via Google Analytics	
Conversion Rate	A percentage Orders divided by Clicks	This should be in line with your website's average Conversion Rate.
Sales	The value of the orders	
AOV	The average order value Sales divided by Orders	Partly depends on what you are promoting in the email, but generally should be online with normal AOVs
Sales per Visitor	A great way to compare the performance of activity where the traffic volume varies Sales divided by delivered	

Different pieces of Partnership activity will come in at different speeds. An email will be done within a week, whereas an order confirmation link may be in place for 12 months – so be sure to compare results fairly.

Successful Partnership Marketing Checklist

- Have clear objectives
- Select the companies to partner with carefully
- Make sure you deliver on your end of the bargain
- Keep looking for new opportunities

NOTES

What are the key points from this section?

Other Notes:

WEBSITE
Visit **eCommerceMasterPlan.com** for the latest information on Partnership Marketing.

Top Tip: An Alternative Form of Partnership: Affiliate Marketing

Affiliate marketing is a method of offering any website a commission on sales they send to you. Generally, it's a very broad piece of activity: you let anyone advertise you, so you are letting go of your brand somewhat.

Whilst a lot of Affiliates are people who have websites on a certain topic that they are looking to monetize, there are also a lot of Voucher Code sites, Cashback sites, and other highly unfocused affiliates.

To tap into this massive marketplace, you need to use one of the big Affiliate Networks. They have all the software and deal with all the money, and give you access to thousands of website owners who may want to advertise your products.

Unlike normal partnering, you don't have much control over what customers are driven to you; with some of my mail order clients I have found that over 70% of all people buying affiliates were already our customers. So it can also be expensive. You will pay a monthly fee to the network, a commission to the affiliates of 5–15%, and a further 3–4% of all sales to the network, too.

But if you have a product that's attractive to many people, this can be a very quick way to generate sales.

Top Tip: An Alternative Form of Partnership: PiggyBacking

Even though PiggyBacking is an eCommerce Business Structure in its own right (two, actually!), it is also a sales method open to all eCommerce Businesses.

See Step 2 for a guide to selecting which PiggyBack websites to partner with.

With PiggyBack Partnering you are picking websites to sell your products through: that might be Amazon, eBay, or someone more niche like MyDeco.

You will pay a PiggyBack partner either a fee structure, or a commission on sales. If your products fit with a PiggyBack site it can be a great way to tap into the visitor traffic that wants your items.

You've read the book, what's next?

You have now built your own eCommerce MasterPlan, so it's time to start implementing. But it's not time to stop learning – eCommerce and online marketing are still evolving so:

- Always keep optimising – optimise your products, your website, your financials, and of course your marketing.
- Keep learning – watch out for new opportunities, and test those you think might work for your business.

I hope you have found the contents of this book useful, and I would love to hear your thoughts. Just go to eCommerceMasterPlan.com and you'll find lots of ways to let me know.

I am committed to keeping eCommerceMasterPlan.com up to date with the information the eCommerce business owner or marketer needs to know. It is simple, sensible advice. Visit today and subscribe to our emails, and follow us on social media.

Most of all – Enjoy it!

Chloë

July 2012

PS please do let me know how you get on – I'd love to hear from you. Email me at chloe@eCommerceMasterPlan.com
PPS turn the page for a special offer to help you Get Started

Half Price: eCommerce MasterPlan: Get Started

This voucher entitles you to 50% off one of our eCommerce MasterPlan: Get Started training days.

Go the website eCommerceMasterPlan.com/GetStarted to find out more and get booked on.

Your Voucher Code: ECMP5

We're always adding more Get Started days, so if you can't see one you can get to, then please sign up to our emails to find out first about the next one.

50%

If you want more help, or want to accelerate your progress even faster...

Chloë is available to speak or consult right now – contact details below
On the website we have details of where Chloë is speaking in the coming months
Chloë's online marketing agency indiumonline can help you with a range of managed online marketing activity see indiumonline.co.uk
For social media training and strategic help – indiumtraining.co.uk can help
Plus you'll find lots of great extra content on eCommerceMasterPlan.com
Watch out for further eCommerce MasterPlan books in 2013

Contact Details:
- **t:** 01865 980 630
- **e:** chloe@ecommercemasterplan.com
- **p:** c/o indium
  Windsor House
  12-14 High St
  Kidlington
  OX5 2DH

Recommended Reading

The following eCommerce-related books I have found both enlightening and enjoyable – these are the ones I don't lend to anyone!

Malmsten, Ernst, *Boo Hoo: A Dot.com Story From Concept to Catastrophe* (Random House, 2002)
The ultimate tale of eCommerce woe; this might have all happened over 10 years ago but many companies are still making the same mistakes today.

Timpson, John, *Upside Down Management: A common sense guide to better business* (John Wiley & Sons, 2010)

This is a very good guide to retailing, with a pragmatic, sensible approach.
Collier, Paul M., *Accounting for Managers: Interpreting accounting information for decision-making* (John Wiley & Sons, 2012)
If you struggle with the numbers, this is the book for you.
Anderson, Chris, *The Long Tail* (Hyperion Books, 2006)
A concept that you need to understand if you are going to succeed online, and so well explained. Read this and you'll see the long tail everywhere.
Godin, Seth, *Poke the Box* (The Domino Project, 2011)
This takes only about 2 hours to read cover to cover, and it's Seth's manifesto for getting on with it, for initiating. It will be on my Kindle forever.

Find out more on eCommerceMasterPlan.com
I'm already building up more content about the different eCommerce Business Structures, and news from the ever-changing world of eCommerce on the website – so visit today to subscribe:

eCommerceMasterPlan.com (including RSS feed and Email Newsletter)

Go on, sign up for more at:

eCommerceMasterPlan.com